CHURCHILL
A Life in Cartoons

Dr Tim Benson is Britain's leading authority on political cartoons. He runs the Political Cartoon Gallery and Café which is located near the River Thames in Putney. He has produced numerous books on the history of cartoons, including *David Low Censored*, *Giles's War*, *Churchill in Caricature*, *Low and the Dictators*, *The Cartoon Century: Modern Britain through the Eyes of its Cartoonists*, *Drawing the Curtain: The Cold War in Cartoons*, *Over the Top: A Cartoon History of Australia at War*, *How to be British: A Cartoon Celebration* and over ten volumes of *Britain's Best Political Cartoons*.

CHURCHILL

A Life in Cartoons

Edited by Tim Benson

HUTCHINSON
◆▬▬◆▬▬◆
HEINEMANN

1 3 5 7 9 10 8 6 4 2

Hutchinson Heinemann
20 Vauxhall Bridge Road
London SW1V 2SA

Hutchinson Heinemann is part of the Penguin Random House group of
companies whose addresses can be found at global.penguinrandomhouse.com

Penguin
Random House
UK

The author wishes to thank Warren Bernard, Dr Ulrich Schnakenberg and
Peter Vanamelsfoort for their help in researching images for this anthology.

Herblock images © Herblock Foundation

Low and Illingworth images © Solo Syndication

First published by Hutchinson Heinemann in 2024

www.penguin.co.uk

A CIP catalogue record for this book is available from the British Library.

ISBN 9781529153286

Printed and bound in Italy by L.E.G.O. S.p.A.

The authorised representative in the EEA is Penguin Random House Ireland,
Morrison Chambers, 32 Nassau Street, Dublin D02 YH68

www.greenpenguin.co.uk

Penguin Random House is committed to a sustainable future
for our business, our readers and our planet. This book is made
from Forest Stewardship Council® certified paper.

Introduction

Following an unrivalled career that spanned sixty years and reached both great heights and depths of political fortune, Sir Winston Churchill undoubtedly became the most caricatured politician in history. From the day he entered Parliament in 1900 through to his retirement from public life in 1964, cartoonists reacted to, and played their part in, the vicissitudes of Churchill's political and military life. From the latter years of the First World War and through the 1920s, Churchill was regularly ridiculed for his perceived misjudgements and follies, most notably the Gallipoli debacle. Churchill's 'wilderness years' followed, spending much of the 1930s out of government due, in part, to his views on India and support for Edward VIII during the Abdication Crisis. Cartoonists who had previously depicted him as a warmonger and an arch-reactionary now ignored him and thought him irrelevant. Lord Beaverbrook, the proprietor of the *Daily Express*, even referred to Churchill as a 'busted flush'. And then, as war once again engulfed Europe, Britain needed a decisive, galvanising leader. Churchill rose again to become Britain's glorious wartime Prime Minister. His finest hour would coincide with that of our nation's cartoonists too. Britain's greatest caricaturists, as well as artists from around the world, visually documented Churchill's war leadership, capturing almost every victory, setback, military manoeuvre and speech and providing an extraordinary record of the war years. For that reason, this

VINTAGE YEAR

A cartoon by John Musgrave-Wood (Emmwood) (30 November 1957, *Daily Mail*) for Churchill's 83rd birthday. 2024 marks 150 years since Churchill's birth.

anthology will primarily focus on Churchill's exploits during the Second World War and the years preceding it.

Though he would come to be one of the most popular politicians to caricature, at the beginning of his political career Churchill suffered, ironically, from a lack of distinctive features. He had not gone completely unnoticed, thanks primarily to his father (the former Chancellor of the Exchequer, Lord Randolph Churchill) but, according to contemporary cartoonists, the younger Churchill had a rather bland appearance. Writing in August 1904, well before Churchill had become famous for his bulldog expression and cigar-chomping habits, Francis Carruthers Gould (Britain's first full-time political cartoonist at a national newspaper) said that Churchill did not have 'the features which lent themselves to easily recognisable conventional treatment as readily as his father's'. Gould bemoaned that young Winston was rather a disappointment: 'Winston Churchill's face is, from the caricaturist's point of view, what I call an elusive one, by which I mean that the more you try to get it the more you lose it, and the likeness which appears with only a few strokes of the pen disappears with elaboration.' However, he did think, somewhat prophetically, that Churchill was still worth watching with interest, 'for the reason that he may one day have to be prominent on the pictorial stage'. The great David Low also noted that the young Churchill did not offer much to the caricaturist. According to Low, Churchill belonged 'to that sandy type which cannot be rendered properly in black lines. His eyes, blue, bulbous and heavy lidded, would be impossible.' Another problem, according to the *Daily Express* cartoonist Sidney Strube, was that Churchill's speeches were too subtle to be of any use to the cartoonist. This would, of

This drawing by Francis Carruthers Gould (27 October 1904, *Westminster Gazette*), captioned 'An Impressionist Sketch', demonstrates his difficulty in capturing a distinctive image of the young Churchill.

course, change significantly by the time of the Second World War, when his speeches, often laden with rich metaphorical pickings, offered ample material for political cartoonists.

The remedy, according to Gould, was that Churchill needed to develop some more distinctive qualities. 'The conclusion of the matter, from the political caricaturist's point of view,' he said, 'is that if a politician has ambition it is important that he should accentuate his personality so that he may be chosen as being easy to represent rather than avoided as being difficult.' Low agreed that Churchill urgently needed to enhance his image. According to Low: 'Statesmen must advertise. Indeed, it is vital to the working of our modern democracy that the persons of political leaders be readily identifiable. Cartoonists and caricaturists have their use in creating or embellishing tags of identity, a fact which is not lost on astute politicians.'

Perhaps heeding their advice, Churchill started wearing a variety of hats, all of which were distinctive in that they were too small for his head. Churchill once claimed that this was a deliberate strategy, beginning in 1910 when he caused a stir by donning a felt cap several sizes too small in front of photographers. Percy Fearon (Poy), cartoonist for the *Evening News*, affirmed that, although he 'had noticed the smallness of his hats long before 1910', it was around this time that the diminutive headwear became something of a trademark. 'At that time the salient feature of my caricatures was the curl on the top of his head. It was only when this vanished prematurely that I turned to the hat and made it the new hallmark.' Churchill reinforced his affiliation with small hats a few years later when addressing the Worshipful Company of Feltmakers. *Punch* reported that Churchill had talked of 'the most essential desideratum of a hat, and that was that it should be too small. Whether it began by being too small or became in time too small depended on the wearer; but there was something smug and cowardly about a hat that fitted. It suggested failure.' By the time Churchill became First Lord of the Admiralty in 1911, the association with odd headgear had succeeded in bringing him to the full attention of cartoonists and therefore the wider public. In 1913 the *Tatler* reported:

Winston Churchill is a boon and a blessing to the cartoonist . . . because his head and body gear are as distinctive as the

'Hats That Have Helped Me. Mr. Winston Churchill (trying on Colonial headgear). "Very becoming – but on the small side, as usual."' Leonard Raven-Hill's cartoon for *Punch* (26 January 1921) proves that Winston had become notorious for his diminutive hats. Churchill was Secretary of State for War and Air at the time but was shortly to be appointed Secretary of State for the Colonies.

man himself. A hat-maker might forgive the broad turned collars or the legging trousers, but the hat, which in shape is what one might call a 'tweenie', between a topper and a bowler, is hard to pardon, while the little Alpine hat which perches perkily on the top of that massive brow is more reminiscent of [comedian] George Robey than a First Lord.

A few months later, the *Daily Chronicle* asked the question: 'Is Winston Churchill setting a new fashion, or is he only playing up to the cartoonists who want a "feature?"' Churchill was thrilled with the attention his hats caused. His son Randolph remarked: 'My father never met a hat he didn't like.'

Of course, by the time of the Second World War, Churchill had consciously added his two most famous tags of identity – the cigar and the 'V for victory' gesture. Despite having smoked cigars since travelling to Cuba in 1895, Churchill now began the habit of always carrying an outsized cigar in public to cultivate an idiosyncratic image for cartoonists and photographers alike. The cigar was almost certainly a prop, as Low had noticed that the cigars he carried in public were 'smoked never more than about one inch'. In July 1941, Churchill used the two-fingered V for victory sign for the first time. However, he initially performed the sign with his palm facing towards him, which gave the signal a much ruder meaning. Churchill had a mischievous sense of humour, but we will never know if this was deliberate. His private secretary, John Colville, wrote at the time in his private diaries: 'The PM will give the V-sign with two fingers in spite of representations repeatedly made to him that this gesture has quite another significance.'

Victor Weisz's (Vicky) cartoon was published in the *News Chronicle* on 23 November 1945. Far from being bland, by the end of the war Churchill had, arguably, become too easy to caricature. The painting refers to Churchill's reputation as an amateur bricklayer – a hobby he picked up while building the walls on his Chartwell estate in 1928.

David Low working on a sketch of Churchill
(brandishing the 'V for Victory' sign) and
Clement Attlee, circa early 1950s.

Part of the rationale behind this curated image may have been that Churchill enjoyed the stark contrast between depictions of himself and Hitler. The Führer was not only a non-smoker, but he also forbade smoking in his company. Following Hitler's lead, the Nazis saw smoking cigars as decadent and self-indulgent and went to great lengths to stamp the habit out. Hitler, unlike Churchill, was also teetotal and so German cartoonists regularly made much of the latter's penchant for alcohol. Perhaps this is one of the many reasons why, according to the *Daily Herald*, Churchill was the Nazis' 'best-hated man', even before he was Prime Minister.

So successful was Churchill in promoting himself during the war that Low felt it unfair the Prime Minister took all the credit. For it was, in Low's opinion, the cartoonist's portrayal of him that successfully emblazoned Churchill in the public mind. 'Don't imagine,' Low cautioned, 'that the familiar wartime idea of Churchill with his V sign and cigar was all his own invention.' The Australian cartoonist Thomas Challen (Tac), who later worked for the *Sunday Pictorial*, agreed that Churchill's attempts at self-promotion had proved a triumph. 'Mr Winston Churchill is the most striking and drawable person in British public life,' he said, 'probably because, from his earliest political days, he has studied his own caricatures, and endeavoured to live up to them.'

It is certainly true that Churchill had a lifelong passion for political cartooning and closely followed contemporary cartoonists' depictions of him. His love of cartoons stemmed from his early boarding school days when on Sundays he was allowed to study volumes of *Punch*, describing them as 'a very good way of learning history'. In the 1920s, while Chancellor of the Exchequer, Churchill was known to regularly cut out cartoons of himself from the newspapers and stick them into annual scrapbooks. In fact, according to David Low: 'Churchill hung all my most vicious works around the Treasury Office.' In June 1931, Churchill even wrote a well-received and thoughtful essay on the subject of political cartoons and cartoonists for the *Strand* magazine. But by the 1930s Churchill was out of government and rarely featured in the press, with or without the small hats. This he obviously regretted, noting:

Just as eels are supposed to get used to skinning, so politicians get used to being caricatured. In fact, by a strange trait in human nature they even get to like it. If we must confess it, they are quite offended and downcast when the cartoons stop. They wonder what has gone wrong, they wonder what they have done amiss . . . they fear old age and obsolescence are creeping upon them. They murmur: 'We are not mauled and maltreated as we used to be. The great days are ended.'

By the time the Second World War had broken out, lack of attention from cartoonists was no longer a problem. Now, Churchill's issue was how to control the cartoonists' representations of him, given the influence they had in mass circulation newspapers. He was not afraid to complain to newspaper proprietors and their editors if he felt cartoons were inappropriate or unfair. One night he got his secretary, Phyllis Moir, out of bed in the middle of the night to take a letter to David Low, complaining: 'You make [Conservative peer] Lord Hailsham and me look exactly alike in your cartoons.' In December 1940, Churchill was furious about a Low cartoon that had made fun of a Labour colleague in the coalition government. In a letter to Lord Beaverbrook (who was both the proprietor of the *Evening Standard* and Minister of Aircraft Production in Churchill's cabinet) he wrote: 'The cartoon in today's *Evening Standard* against [Arthur] Greenwood will certainly make your path and mine more stony. I know the difficulty with Low, but others do not, and cartoons in your papers showing your colleagues in ridiculous guise will cause fierce resentment.' The 'difficulty' Churchill referred to was that Low's contract prevented any editorial interference in his cartoons. His caricatures often went against

A Sid Moon cartoon published in the *Daily Sketch* on 26 October 1941. The newspaper commented that Churchill's 'principal contribution to the war is to shout for action – by somebody else'. They later received a letter from Churchill's personal secretary saying that 'The Prime Minister is much struck by the excellent cartoon . . . Would you please let me know if the original is available for purchase?' The 'exemption' refers to the September 1940 Fire Watchers Order which compelled men to watch out for incendiary bombs and put out small fires during raids.

the paper's political leanings – and regularly frustrated both Beaverbrook and Churchill – but there was little they could do about it. Churchill, however, still remonstrated with Beaverbrook in his belief that such attacks would cause 'all those ministers conceiving themselves threatened to bank up against you and your projects, and owing to my friendship with you they will think that I am condoning the attacks made upon them. He does you and your work disservice by these cartoons, and he is too well aware of what he does.' On such occasions Beaverbrook always denied control over Low, stating that it was 'a matter of real grief'. 'I do not know how to deal with the situation,' he said. 'I do not agree with Low. I have rarely done so. I do not interfere with Low. I have never done so.' Beaverbrook would later complain: 'I had two artists on my hands. One at night-time – that was the Prime Minister complaining about Low. The other in the morning – that was Low complaining about Churchill.'

Churchill seemed to have something of a love-hate relationship with Low. Churchill once praised Low as 'a great master of black and white; he is the Charlie Chaplin of caricature, and tragedy and comedy are the same to him'. Churchill was known to keep and display Low's cartoons. But there were also times when Churchill bitterly attacked Low as a 'scoundrel', whom he said 'never drew a single line in praise of England'. But Churchill's ire was not reserved for David Low alone. By 1942, Churchill had become increasingly frustrated with other left-wing cartoonists for continuing to criticise his government's running of the war. Philip Zec was severely reprimanded for a cartoon published in the *Daily Mirror* on 6 March 1942, which Churchill saw as a

'*Winterton's Nightmare.*' One of David Low's more critical cartoons for the *Evening Standard* (21 May 1942). According to the cartoonist, 'The British House of Commons debated whether the control of the war should be by a committee of Chiefs of Staff headed by the Minister of Defence, Churchill, or whether it should be concentrated in one man, Churchill. Some members thought such a concentration existed already.' On 19 May, Earl Winterton complained in the House of Commons that Churchill was acting as a one-man government. Clement Attlee chastised Winterton for implying that the Prime Minister was acting as 'some kind of dictator'.

direct attack on his government. At around this time he also wrote to Lord Layton, chairman of the *News Chronicle*, in regard to a cartoon by Victor Weisz (Vicky). 'I chanced to see the enclosed cartoon and thought it quite outside ordinary limits. I was astonished that a newspaper you control should harbour it.' In a subsequent attack on the press, which was specifically aimed at the tabloids and cartoonists such as Low, Zec and Vicky, Churchill declared that 'our affairs are not conducted entirely by simpletons and dunderheads as the comic papers try to depict'. Even *Punch* was not immune from such attacks; Churchill was still a regular and ardent reader of the magazine, but he had not forgiven its pro-Appeasement stance before the war. In a letter to the editor in April 1943, Churchill wrote that he was 'a constant reader of *Punch* over so many years,' but that one of its recent cartoons was 'the biggest flop since the cartoon of John Bull waking from his wartime nightmare on the very day the Germans marched on Prague.' He concluded, 'I am sure your colleagues will welcome criticism from their readers.'

The Conservatives lost the general election of 1945 and Churchill became Leader of the Opposition for six years before being re-elected as Prime Minister in 1951 at the age of almost seventy-seven. In February 1954, Leslie Illingworth drew a cartoon for *Punch* of the Prime Minister, listless at his desk, the face registering the unmistakable effects of a partial paralysis he had suffered as the result of a stroke the preceding summer. The caption was taken from Psalm 114: 'Man goeth forth unto his work and to his labour until the evening.' Churchill was bitterly hurt by the cartoon. 'Yes, there's malice in it. Look at my hands – I have beautiful hands ... *Punch*

Leslie Illingworth's cartoon for *Punch* (3 February 1954).

goes everywhere. I shall have to retire if this sort of thing goes on.' Churchill's doctor, Lord Moran, was also shocked by what he considered a vicious caricature of the Prime Minister. 'There was something un-English in this savage attack on his failing powers,' he commented. 'The eyes were dull and lifeless. There was no tone in the flaccid muscles; the jowl sagged. It was the expressionless mask of extreme old age.' Churchill finally retired as Prime Minister in April the following year, ironically during a newspaper strike so there were no cartoons of him leaving Downing Street.

Churchill's daughter, Mary Soames, once told me that while she was growing up at Chartwell she was 'mystified' by what she deemed to be cruel and callous cartoons of her father hanging around the house. She thought that he would be hurt by them, but was surprised to find that he appreciated and even enjoyed them. Indeed, there appeared to be genuine respect and admiration between the statesman and many of his caricaturists. Many cartoonists were saddened by his leaving office. The prime ministers that followed never quite matched the visual greatness that he had offered over such a long career. Sidney Strube, for his part, once commented: 'If Churchill had retired at fifty we would probably have already lost the war.' As an artist in his own right, Churchill greatly admired political cartoonists and their work. Even David Low once noted: 'Winston is very interested in caricature and will yarn for hours on the technical side of art . . . he had a genuine appreciation of quality in caricatural draughtsmanship.' More than that, from courting the cartoonists' attention with his bizarre millinery in his early career, to both collecting and critiquing cartoons featuring his likeness while in office,

Churchill's daughter Mary Soames at the Political Cartoon Gallery in 2007 looking at the Illingworth *Punch* cartoon which so upset her father.

'To Winston, from his old friend and castigator.' David Low created this cartoon, showing Churchill being feted by his younger selves, for *Illustrated* magazine to mark Churchill's 80th birthday in 1954. The occasional adversaries clearly had the greatest respect for one another.

Churchill clearly appreciated that cartoonists reflected and informed the political landscape of the day. Churchill is, of course, remembered and celebrated for his wartime leadership, but he was made iconic by the cigar-chewing, siren-suited, bulldog-like persona that contemporary cartoonists helped to create – a character that has lived on, long after the man himself.

Victor Weisz (Vicky) celebrated Churchill's 70th birthday with this cartoon for the *News Chronicle* on 30 November 1944.

1914–20

'There be land-rats and water-rats.' – Shakespeare

A sermon to the German from a firm 'un.

Churchill had been appointed to the post of First Lord of the Admiralty in 1911 and played a pivotal role in readying the Royal Navy for conflict. When the First World War broke out in August 1914, the Navy utilised its overwhelming sea power to transport more than 120,000 troops to France and blockade Germany's North Sea ports. Addressing the crowd at a recruiting meeting at Liverpool, Churchill said: 'We hope a decision at sea will be a feature of this war. Our men, who are spending a tireless vigil, hope that they will have a chance to settle the question with the German fleet; and if they do not come out and fight they will be dug out like rats in a hole.'

1 September 1914, Matthew Sandford (Matt), *Daily Dispatch*

From our criminals' album: Winston Churchill, pirate;
Nikolai Nikolaevich, millionaire fraudster.

Churchill sent a British submarine flotilla to assist the Russian navy in blockading German ports on the Baltic Sea, in addition to the Royal Navy patrol in the North Sea. They established a list of contraband, including food, which could not be imported into Germany, thereby preventing almost all trade from the US and any shipments of Swedish iron ore – acts which the German press saw as thievery.

Grand Duke Nikolai Nikolaevich, who was 6 foot 6 tall, was cousin to Tsar Nicholas II and commander-in-chief of the Russian army during the first year of war.

13 September 1914, Olaf Gulbransson,
Simplicissimus **(Munich, Germany)**

Churchill (after losing three cruisers): 'The Germans seem to have misunderstood my principle of three English ships to one German!'

On 22 September, the Royal Navy suffered one of the worst disasters in its history. Three armoured cruisers, HMS *Hogue*, HMS *Aboukir* and HMS *Cressy*, patrolling in the southern North Sea, were sunk by a German U-boat. More than 1,450 sailors, mostly reservists, were killed. The events shook confidence in Churchill's Navy and awakened the Allies to the dangers of enemy submarines.

In 1912, in response to a new German naval law that significantly expanded its fleet, Churchill had promised that two British vessels would be built for every ship produced by Germany.

26 September 1914, Walter Trier, *Lustige Blätter* **(Berlin, Germany)**

Prime Minister Herbert Asquith created a War Council comprised of himself, Churchill, David Lloyd George (Chancellor of the Exchequer), Edward Grey (Foreign Secretary) and Lord Kitchener (Secretary of State for War). Aside from this council, Asquith mostly followed a 'business as usual' approach to government. On 9 November, the Australian light cruiser HMAS *Sydney* had sunk the German cruiser SMS *Emden*, which had previously sunk twenty-five civilian ships and shelled the ports of Madras, India, and Penang, British Malaya. Churchill sent a message to the Australian crew: 'Warmest congratulations on the brilliant entry of the Australian Navy into the war, and the signal service rendered to the Allied cause.'

11 November 1914, Matthew Sandford (Matt), *Daily Dispatch*

After the Battle of Heligoland [Bight]. Beatty: Stupid thing, Sir, our 'Lion' is torn up, our 'Tiger' is gone . . . !

Churchill: Never mind, my dear, the public won't notice!

This cartoon reflects false reports, published in the German press, of a victory for the Central Powers at the Battle of Dogger Bank on 24 January. The battle was in fact a victory for the Royal Navy (led by Vice-Admiral Sir David Beatty), which intercepted a German raiding squadron and sunk SMS *Blücher* with the loss of more than 900 men. HMS *Lion*, the flagship, and HMS *Tiger* did take fire but the ships returned to port and only fifteen men were lost.

6 February 1915, Walter Trier, *Lustige Blätter* **(Berlin, Germany)**

4

A ROLAND

FOR THEIR OLIVER.

In response to the British blockade of German ports, Admiral Hugo von Pohl, commander of the German High Seas Fleet, announced on 4 February a policy of 'unrestricted submarine warfare'. The waters around Great Britain were now considered a war zone and, from 18 February onwards, every enemy merchant vessel in this zone would be attacked without warning.

The phrase 'A Roland for their Oliver' means tit-for-tat, or blow-for-blow.

17 February 1915, J. M. Staniforth, *Western Mail*

A victim of vapour

*Irate patient: 'This is ruining my system. Turn
off the tap or I'll murder somebody.'*

Suave attendant: 'Ah, I feels it! Now for a little more pressure.'

Speaking in the House of Commons on 15 February, Churchill responded to the threat of unrestricted submarine warfare by warning that 'Germany cannot be allowed to adopt a system of open piracy and murder ... the full force of naval pressure [is to be applied] to the enemy.'

19 February 1915, Matthew Sandford (Matt), *Daily Dispatch*

Churchill's flag fraud

*Britannia: 'With this shabby garb I can no
longer trust myself to go out.'*
*Churchill: 'Cheer up, old lady. If you must,
steal a better outfit for yourself.'*

The German press widely reported that the British Government had secretly ordered its merchant vessels to fly the flag of neutral nations, including the United States, to avoid recognition by German U-boats.

**23 February 1915, Thomas Heine,
Simplicissimus (Munich, Germany)**

A pet aversion

[After the picture by Phiz, in 'The Old Curiosity Shop', of Quilp and Kit's effigy.] Mr Winston Churchill has a prominent place in the hate of British ministers expressed in Germany.

The cartoon mocks the ire that the German press reserved for Winston Churchill as the political head of the Royal Navy. By 1915 the naval blockade caused Germany's imports to fall by 55 per cent from their pre-war levels, which meant that a rationing system was introduced.

The cartoon references the scene from Dickens' *The Old Curiosity Shop* in which the malicious dwarf Daniel Quilp takes out his frustrations on an old ship's figurehead.

25 February 1915, F. Carruthers Gould, *Westminster Gazette*

WILLY STIEBORSKY

Rat-catcher Churchill: 'We're seeking out the German
ships like rats from their hideouts!'

Following the declaration of unrestricted submarine warfare, the number of attacks against Allied ships steadily increased. The German press took delight in recalling Churchill's earlier remarks in 1914 that, if the German navy did not come out and fight, they would be 'dug out like rats in a hole'.

11 March 1915, Willy Stieborsky, *Die Muskete* **(Vienna, Austria)**

*After work. Churchill: 'Oh God, it's not easy being
the English Navy minister all day long!'*

The *Illustrated London News*, a weekly magazine published
during the First World War, commented that this cartoon,
portraying Churchill as a weary ass, was 'Germany trying to
be funny'. 'German humour,' it continued, 'is dealt out with a
heavy hand, first-cousin to the historical mailed fist [the threat
of armed force]. Delicate satire is to them "unknown."'

The cartoon may refer to the phrase 'lions led by donkeys' used
to describe soldiers led to their deaths by inept commanders.

13 March 1915, Walter Trier, *Lustige Blätter* **(Berlin, Germany)**

John Bull learning his real strength at last.

This patriotic cartoon shows John Bull, the national personi-
fication of the United Kingdom, building up his strength.
The dumb-bells feature the likenesses of Churchill and
Lord Kitchener, who, as Secretary of State for War, was the
political head of the military.

27 March 1915, Alfred Leete, *London Opinion*

The Optimist

Mr Churchill: 'Excellent, gentlemen! I want to put together a report straight away that the tobacco shortage in England has now finally been resolved.'

Our U-boats provide the crew of the steamers with cigars.

Germany's mercilessly effective campaign against merchant ships continued apace. In the first month of unrestricted submarine warfare, twenty-nine ships and nearly 90,000 tons of cargo were sunk. It was alleged that one U-boat commander had remarked to a captain of a French ship before it was torpedoed: 'Give my compliments to Lord Churchill!' Tobacco was a significant import during the First World War, as troops were supplied with a ration of two ounces per day.

Churchill, it seems, had already become synonymous with the cigar.

27 March 1915, Franz Jüttner, *Lustige Blätter* (Berlin, Germany)

The 'Blue Riband'

In the tug-of-war between Germany and England, Churchill 'lists' heavily.

On 7 May, the ocean liner RMS *Lusitania* (which held the Blue Riband accolade for the fastest Atlantic crossing in 1908) was torpedoed by a German submarine off the coast of Ireland with the loss of 1,198 lives. The German press hailed this a major victory for Admiral Tirpitz, Secretary of State of the German Imperial Navy. But the sinking provoked the ire of the Americans. US President Woodrow Wilson issued an ultimatum that any further sinkings would be seen as 'deliberately unfriendly'. In the UK, throngs of men rushed to enlist. Churchill said of the sinking: 'The poor babies who perished in the ocean struck a blow at German power more deadly than could have been achieved by the sacrifice of 100,000 men.'

22 May 1915, artist unknown, *Lustige Blätter* **(Berlin, Germany)**

THE COMBINED CONCERT COMPANY.

FIRST PIERROT: "Ladies and gentlemen—a character-song entitled: 'Arf a mo', Kaiser!'"

On 25 May, Asquith stunned Churchill by demoting him to Chancellor of the Duchy of Lancaster. Churchill had helped orchestrate the Dardanelles campaign and plan the military landings at Gallipoli. In March three battleships were sunk by Turkish mines and 600 sailors were killed. Lord Fisher, First Sea Lord, resigned after bitter arguments with Churchill over the campaign. Due to the controversy, Asquith's Liberals were forced into a coalition government. Nine Conservatives entered government, including Andrew Bonar Law as Secretary of State for Colonies, Austen Chamberlain as Secretary of State for India and Arthur Balfour as the new First Lord of the Admiralty.

Pierrot is a sad clown from pantomime.

27 May 1915, Matthew Sandford (Matt), *Daily Dispatch*

ARE WE D———D ?
The answer is in the negative.

In his first appearance since leaving the Admiralty, Churchill gave what was reported as an 'uplifting' speech to his constituents in Dundee. He gave his support to the continuation of the Dardanelles expedition: 'Through the Narrows of the Dardanelles and across the ridges of the Gallipoli Peninsula lie some of the shortest paths to a triumphant peace.' He also urged listeners: 'Gather afresh in heart and spirit all the energies of your being, bend anew together for a supreme effort . . . the might of Britain hurled united into the conflict will be irresistible.'

7 June 1915, Matthew Sandford (Matt), *Daily Dispatch*

A popular song

*But Fiddle-de-dee sings clear and loud./ And his trills
and his quavers astonish the crowd./ Such a singer
as he/ You'll nowhere see;/ They'll all be screaming
for Fiddle-de-dee! – The Ingoldsby Legends.*

Churchill's optimistic speech in Dundee was widely praised
but was matched by anxiety in other quarters of the
Government. On 4 June, British, French and Indian forces
lost some 6,500 men after attempting to capture the Ottoman
defences at Achi Baba. In the second week of June, the Royal
Navy sustained heavy losses on Cape Helles, Gallipoli. The
Shell Crisis, a shortage of artillery shells on the front lines,
was at its peak and David Lloyd George had been appointed to
the new post of Minister of Munitions to manage the crisis.

8 June 1915, J. M. Staniforth, *Western Mail*

*Winston: 'This is free and easy, at any rate.
And there's room for expansion.'*

*That Mr. Winston Churchill will become Minister
of Aviation is a theme of persistent discussion.*

Churchill had long had a fascination with, and belief in the
future of, aviation. He had learned to fly and in his time at
the Admiralty had renewed focus on the Royal Naval Air
Service. By summer 1915, he hoped he would be appointed
minister of a special air department, but nothing came of it.
According to the *Daily Mail*: 'A Minister of Aviation is the
crying need of the moment, and the name of Mr Churchill
leaps into the mind. In such a position, Mr Churchill would
be afforded scope for that genius which delights in action and
attack . . . [he] is wasted in the musty and archaic office of
the Duchy of Lancaster.'

21 June 1915, Matthew Sandford (Matt), *Daily Dispatch*

The Battle of the Ships (from the new Iliad)

*'Behold, the devastating battle rages among the ships,/ But
Churchilles, he keeps his garrulous mouth shut and growls./
The huge embarrassment lies open before the world./ Nobody
covers it up any more, because Churchilles is silent.*

By June 1915 Churchill has fallen out of favour. He was still
a member of the War Council but his opinions had no force
and he was often left out of military and naval discussions. In
July he wrote to a friend: 'I do not want office, but only war
direction . . . I am profoundly unsettled and cannot use my
gift.' Without a department to run, Churchill found a weekend
retreat at Hoe Farm in Surrey and took up painting.

11 July 1915, Arthur Johnson, *Kladderadatsch* (Berlin, Germany)

'Promising.'

(Mr. Churchill's Art is promising, but lacks something in execution. – Vide Daily Press.)

Churchill's reputation had sunk so low that even the British press mocked him for his optimistic, yet unsuccessful, ideas.

'The Hornet Swarm' alludes to an early notion of Churchill's that Zeppelins could be attacked by a 'swarm of hornets' (aeroplanes armed with bombs and guns), although, at the time, aeroplanes could not reach the necessary altitude for this to work. 'The Ace' refers to the fort at Kilid Bahr on the Dardanelles, which was known as 'Ace of Spades' and is symbolic of the Gallipoli campaign. 'Study of Rats' refers to Churchill's earlier promise to dig out the German High Seas Fleet 'like rats in a hole', only to have U-boats destroy three Royal Navy ships a few weeks later.

30 October 1915, Charles Crombie, *Passing Show*

Then farewell! my trim-built wherry/ Oars, and coat, and badge, farewell!/ Never more (for the present) at Minster Ferry/ Shall your Winston take a spell.

On 6 November, Churchill asked Asquith to make him Governor-General of British East Africa. His request was refused. On 11 November, a new inner cabinet was created, a small policy-making body of five ministers from which Churchill was excluded. That day, Churchill offered his resignation saying he did not feel able 'to remain in well-paid activity'. He decided to join his regiment in France and, on 18 November, left London for the Western Front in uniform.

The caption is based on a song written by Charles Dibdin for his ballad opera, *The Waterman*.

21 November 1915, J. M. Staniforth, *News of the World*

'*Malbrouk s'en va-t-en guerre.*'

And it won't be long, we expect, before things begin to hum, under the Churchill touch.

On 20 November Churchill joined the 2nd Battalion Grenadier Guards as it began a twelve-day spell in the trenches. He wrote to his mother: 'I am happy here . . . I always get on with soldiers . . . Do you know I am quite young again?'

Malbrough [or *Malbrouk*] *s'en va-t-en guerre* is a French folk song lamenting the death in 1722 of John Churchill, 1st Duke of Marlborough. The duke, ancestor of Winston's, was a famed soldier and statesman known for having never lost a battle.

24 November 1915, E. T. Reed, *Bystander*

Lord Fisher and Mr. Churchill

Discouraging an ill-timed outburst

In his resignation speech to the House of Commons on
15 November, Churchill emphasised that all naval experts
in the Admiralty, including Lord Fisher, had believed in the
Dardanelles campaign. He said that 'the naval attack on the
Dardanelles was a naval plan, made by naval authorities
. . . [not] a civilian plan foisted by a political amateur upon
reluctant officers'. The next day Lord Fisher made a statement
in the House of Lords, saying: 'It is unfitting to make personal
explanations affecting national interests when my country is
in the midst of a great war.'

27 November 1915, Bert Thomas, *London Opinion*

Bringing their pom-pom into action

During the winter of 1915–16, Churchill was temporarily promoted to the role of lieutenant-colonel of the 6th Battalion, Royal Scots Fusiliers. He led his men for three and a half months at the front and was well-respected for his attention to detail and good humour. By May 1916, the losses in his battalion had become so severe that it was amalgamated with another division, and Churchill chose to return to the House of Commons. On 23 May, he spoke in the Commons of the unfair burden placed on soldiers in the trenches when so many soldiers, particularly officers, never went near the front line. It was, he said, 'one of the clearest and grimmest class distinctions ever drawn in this world'.

25 May 1916, J. M. Staniforth, *Western Mail*

After Landseer's well-known picture

Churchill continued to be vocal in the House of Commons and, during a vote on 31 May, he spoke of the Government's failure to use the country's resources in the most effective way. His criticisms were seen as an attack on the Secretary of State for War, Lord Kitchener, who was held in the highest esteem by the general public. The day after this cartoon was published, Kitchener was drowned when his ship hit a minefield en route to a secret meeting in Russia.

The cartoon is based on the famous painting by Sir Edwin Landseer entitled *Dignity and Impudence*.

4 June 1916, Edward Huskinson, *People*

They believed that Britain would be unready and easily bullied into peace. But in one sphere, at least, we were fully prepared. The Navy, under Mr Churchill, did all that we expected of it, and that the Willies failed to anticipate.

In his time at the Admiralty, Churchill had overseen the development of new ships, better weapons, a naval aviation service and an oil-powered fleet. By 1916, although Churchill had long been blamed for the failure of the Dardanelles campaign, his success in preparing for war was being recognised.

Haselden had great success depicting Kaiser Wilhelm II and his son Wilhelm in his wartime comic strip, 'The Sad Experiences of Big and Little Willie'. A testament to its popularity was that a prototype of the first British tank was called Little Willie.

14 November 1916, William Haselden, *Daily Mirror*

'Where did that one go?'

With apologies to Capt. Bruce Bairnsfather.

On 9 March, the report of the Dardanelles Commission was released. It offered a ruthless analysis of the Gallipoli campaign's many failings and made clear that Asquith and Kitchener had approved the campaign plans. But Churchill felt that it failed to answer many of the charges laid against him. He wrote a bitter letter to David Lloyd George, complaining: 'The Government excisions in the Dardanelles Report are extremely injurious to me.'

12 March 1917, Percy Fearon (Poy), *Evening News*

Taboo!

Senior member of the Air Board (as Winston is ushered in):
'S-SH! HERE HE COMES!! NOW DO REMEMBER
WHATEVER YOU SAY, DON'T MENTION
"RATS", "HORNETS", OR "WINDBAGS"!' [It has
been rumoured in the Press that Mr. Winston Churchill
is to be appointed Chairman of the Air Board.]

David Lloyd George had outmanoeuvred Asquith and become Prime Minister by December 1916. Lloyd George was better disposed towards Churchill and privately suggested that he could be given an office once the Dardanelles report was published. On 3 June the *Sunday Times* reported the rumour that Churchill was to be made Chairman of the Air Board but commented that 'he would be a grave danger to the Administration and the Empire as a whole'.

The Irish Unionist Party leader, Sir Edward Carson, had recently described Churchill in the *Edinburgh Evening News* as a 'windbag, thinking only of himself'.

23 June 1917, E. T. Reed, *Passing Show*

The "Legitimate Gambler"

John Bull (to the 'unsinkable' Winston): 'Look here, young man! Just you get on with your own job!'

Churchill returned to the Government as Minister of Munitions, but still displayed a preoccupation with the Navy. He submitted a long memorandum to the War Cabinet, 'Naval War Policy, 1917', advocating a scheme to combine the Allied fleets and then divide these into a Blue Water Fleet (which would maintain the blockade of Germany) and a Hazard Fleet (to undertake offensive operations on a great scale). The United States had entered the war in April and, with the addition of the US navy, Churchill calculated that two complete battle fleets could be formed, each more powerful than the German fleet.

15 August 1917, E. T. Reed, *Bystander*

*Churchill: We will smoke out the Germans like rats
out of holes . . . so that we can hide in them!*

By the summer of 1917, Germany had developed the huge, long-distance Gotha bomber aircraft. On 13 June, Gothas carried out their first daylight raid on London. Seventy-two bombs were dropped within a one-mile radius of Liverpool Street Station, causing 162 deaths and injuring 426 civilians. Eighteen children were killed at a primary school in Poplar. It was the highest death toll of any air raid on Britain in the First World War.

2 September 1917, cartoonist unknown,
***Kladderadatsch* (Berlin, Germany)**

The return to the fold
*'Leave them alone and they'll come home,
Bringing their tails behind them.'*

As Minister of Munitions, Churchill had negotiated an end to strikes by engineering workers in munitions factories along the Clyde in 1917. But fresh strikes involving thousands of munitions workers commenced in 1918, threatening a slump in tank production. At Churchill's urging, it was announced that all striking workers would be liable to be sent to the front. The strike collapsed and tank production resumed.

31 July 1918, J. M. Staniforth, *Western Mail*

Winston Churchill: 'Come on, John, another big drink wouldn't do you any harm.'

John Bull: 'Yes; but aren't you making me take too much?'

Following the end of the First World War, Churchill was made Secretary of State for War and Air. In these posts, he announced that the estimated expenditure for the British Army in 1919–20 would be £440 million. *The Times* reported: 'The size of the Estimates presented by Mr. Churchill . . . has frightened many good souls, but there is one thing that cannot fairly be said about them. They are not the Estimates of peace.'

15 March 1919, Bert Thomas, *London Opinion*

Winnie's need!

Churchill: 'If one is the greatest War Minister the World has known, obviously one must have some wars in which to prove it!'

As Secretary of State for War and Air, Churchill was in charge of the massive task of demobilisation. Under Churchill's plans, one million men remained conscripted for an army of occupation on the Rhine needed to extract 'the just terms which the Allies demand'. He also initially opposed the demobilisation of the German army and supported sending British troops to Russia, thinking both would be needed to oppose the new Communist state.

14 May 1919, Will Dyson, *Daily Herald*

1914–1919

THE SUCCESSOR

Even after an exhausting and costly war against Germany, Churchill's support for intervention in Russia was unpopular. According to the *Daily Herald*: 'Winston Churchill is known as the gambler of Antwerp and Gallipoli; his is the imperialist mind behind the new war in Russia . . . He worked for and secured a political position, which he has used to hold in the Army men who have been at the Front since 1916. It is 1919 now! . . . The working class must choose between liberty and Churchill.'

15 May 1919, Will Dyson, *Daily Herald*

Which way, Winston?

Why does Winston keep us guessing/ What he means when he's 'progressing'?/ Is he going to or fro?/ That's the thing we want to know!

Churchill went back and forth on whether to intervene in the Russian Civil War. He initially supported sending the 14,000 British troops left in Russia to unite with anti-Communist forces, believing that of 'all the tyrannies in history, the Bolshevik tyranny is the worst'. He also supported sending munitions and supplies to the Tsarist forces led by Anton Denikin. Following a mutiny in the Russian forces, however, it was clear that British troops should be withdrawn.

27 September 1919, Frank Holland, *John Bull*

A collector of white elephants

Churchill had been obsessed by Russia for much of the year, but the last British troops left the port of Archangel (an anti-Bolshevik stronghold that British and American troops had helped to defend) by October and by the end of the year Denikin's forces were in disarray. It was the latest in a series of military failures that Churchill had been seen to misjudge, and he was now considered something of a political liability.

The term 'white elephant' refers to a possession that is troublesome and difficult to dispose of.

27 September 1919, Alfred Leete, *London Opinion*

'So THAT'S the idea you've got under your little hat, is it?'

A Labour Party delegation to Russia in June 1920 brought
back a document that gave an account of an interview
between Churchill and the anti-Communist emissary General
Golovin in May 1919. It showed that Churchill had promised
the general every possible assistance in support of the anti-
Bolshevik cause, even at the expense of the British taxpayer.
Labour politician Ramsay MacDonald wrote: 'If Mr Churchill
had been an unlimited monarch, he could not have spent the
money and lives of the nation with more unstinted generosity.'

5 July 1920, David Low, *Star*

1931–39

Hallowe'en

Churchill lost his Dundee seat in the 1922 election but was re-elected in 1924 when he stood as a Conservative – and Constitutionalist – candidate for Epping. He then served as Chancellor of the Exchequer under Stanley Baldwin until 1929. By the time of the 1931 election, economic crises persuaded the Conservatives, Liberals and National Labour to form a cross-party National Government. The Conservatives won the most seats, but Ramsay MacDonald (the former Labour leader) stayed on as Prime Minister. Having publicly nicknamed MacDonald the 'Boneless Wonder', it was no surprise that Churchill was passed over for a Cabinet post.

**31 October 1931, Charles Gordon McClure
(Dyke White),** *Daily Record*

In the Commons to-day, Mr. Churchill is to lead
the demand for 'adequate air defences.'

Churchill was out of political office for much of the 1930s – a period that become known as his 'wilderness years'. Even so, he remained vocal on military issues, especially aviation. By 1934, led by Hitler and in violation of the Treaty of Versailles, Germany was building a powerful, well-equipped air force while Britain pressed forward with a policy of disarmament. On 28 November, Churchill gave a speech in the Commons in which he urged the Government to double or even treble spending on air force expansion: 'The flying peril is not a peril from which one can fly . . . We ought to decide now to maintain, at all costs, in the next ten years an air force substantially stronger than that of Germany.'

28 November 1934, Cecil Orr, *Daily Record*

Duet on the air

We like the way you say Good night, Winnie.

(The Defence Debate dispelled the alarmist warnings of Mr. Winston Churchill).

In his Commons speech on 28 November, Churchill had spoken dramatically of a potential aircraft attack as 'menace which no generation before our own has faced, which shakes the very fabric and structure of all our civilised arrangements'. Lord President of the Council, Stanley Baldwin, responded by playing down Churchill's warnings: 'I say that there is no ground at this moment for undue alarm and still less for panic. There is no immediate menace confronting us.' He added that 'should an emergency develop . . . we shall not be caught unprepared'.

30 November 1934, George Middleton, *Birmingham Gazette*

P.C. CHURCHILL: 'Hi, Speed-hound – you are exceeding the limit. You are going too fast and too far!'

Churchill spent much of the early 1930s arguing against making any concessions that might weaken Britain's imperial control over India. But public and political opinion was quickly coming round to the idea that some form of self-government was both inevitable and right, making Churchill seem out-of-touch. In December, Churchill attempted to stall the India Bill (which would give a large measure of autonomy to the provinces of India while still ultimately being controlled by Britain) but was supported by only seventy-five Conservative MPs, leaving the Government with a majority of 238.

Lord Salisbury (the figure on Churchill's right) was one of the most prominent opponents of Indian Home Rule in the Lords, supporting the campaign waged in the Commons by Churchill against the Home Rule legislation.

4 December 1934, Will Dyson, *Daily Herald*

*Our artist thinks he knows how Mr. Winston Churchill secures
his information regarding Germany's rearmaments.*

Churchill continued to warn of the risks posed by German rearmament, and his contacts both at home and abroad fed him information which he used to attack the government's failure to meet the threat. Churchill's main source was Ralph Wigram, a friend and rising star at the Foreign Office. Churchill later wrote of Wigram, 'He saw as clearly as I did, but with more certain information, the awful peril which was closing in upon us . . . Like other officials of high rank, he spoke to me with complete confidence. All this helped me to form and fortify my opinion about the Hitler movement. For my part, with the many connections I now had in France, in Germany, and other countries, I had been able to send him a certain amount of information which we examined together.'

21 January 1935, Cecil Orr, *Daily Record*

'Well, Winston is still there!'

On 11 February, after the second reading of the India Bill, Churchill once again warned against self-government in India. He said he hoped that the British in India were 'forever', as 'honoured partners with our Indian fellow-subjects' but, nevertheless, the bill passed by 404 votes to 133. Lord Salisbury commented that Churchill had 'entirely lost parliamentary touch'.

The British Empire had once been known as 'the Empire on which the sun never sets'.

12 February 1935, Will Dyson, *Daily Herald*

The debate on the Government's defence loan scheme continues to-day.

Neville Chamberlain became Chancellor of the Exchequer in 1931. His initial budgets cut defence spending, but by 1935 an increasingly militarised Germany convinced him of the need to rearm, especially investing in the Royal Air Force. In a debate on 17 February 1937, the Commons agreed to the borrowing of £400 million for defence spending for the next five years. Chamberlain denied that the proposals formed a 'war measure'. Churchill welcomed the increases but asked the barbed question: 'Can you be sure that your programmes, so tardily adopted, will, in fact, be executed in time?'

18 February 1937, Cecil Orr, *Daily Record*

The branded shop

Chamberlain was appointed Prime Minister in May 1937, but his leadership suffered a blow in early 1938 when his Foreign Secretary, Anthony Eden, resigned in protest at the Government's appeasement of Italy. Italy had been isolated after its invasion of Ethiopia, but Chamberlain felt it necessary to enter into negotiations with Mussolini to reduce tension on the continent. During the Eden resignation debate, Churchill said: 'This has been a good week for dictators ... Signor Mussolini has won.' He recognised that Chamberlain had acted to preserve peace but asked: 'What price shall we all have to pay for this?'

24 February 1938, Kimon Evan Marengo (Kem), *Daily Herald*

Stealing his thunder

Neville: My dear Winston, I wish you wouldn't try to terrify me when I'm trying to look terrifying. [Whilst the Prime Minister referred to our almost terrifying power, Mr. Churchill said that Germany's Air Force may be double that of ours.]

During a debate in the Commons on 7 March, Churchill criticised the slowness of the Air Force expansion programme, stating it would 'not surprise me at all if Germany were going to spend in 1938 more than twice as much upon their air force as we . . . Therefore, one may apprehend that German air power was at least double that of ours, and is being expanded at least at double our rate . . . I am bound to say that I feel a very great deal of disquiet . . . that the former position of the Government in regard to parity is now no longer maintained or argued.'

9 March 1938, George Middleton, *Nottingham Journal*

Ah, 'all things come to those who wait,'/ (I say these words to make me glad),/ But something answers soft and sad,/ 'They come, but often come too late.'

After Hitler's forces had marched into Austria on 12 March, a bewildered Chamberlain failed to comprehend why friendlier moves towards Mussolini had not led to Italian support in opposition to Hitler. The division over appeasement led to some in Whitehall calling for Churchill's inclusion in the Cabinet (Churchill was now agitating for the Government to aid Czechoslovakia if, as seemed likely, it was the next victim of an unprovoked attack). But, as the great cartoonist David Low informs us, this was unlikely to happen: 'Churchill's appointment would have distressed "our friends in Italy and Germany". Some scorn was poured on the Churchill "theatrical attitude" as opposed to the Chamberlain "settled purpose of peace".'

23 March 1938, Edward Hynes, *Daily Herald*

In the Back-wash

'Racing at Henley is becoming too feminine.' – Sporting Authority

By September, Chamberlain was in the midst of talks with Hitler and Mussolini that eventually led to the Munich Agreement (permitting Germany to annex the Sudetenland in Czechoslovakia). Churchill, his son-in-law Duncan Sandys MP, Anthony Eden and Duff Cooper (who had been the only minister to resign over the agreement) stood firm in their opposition to appeasement. Churchill would say of the Munich Agreement: 'We have sustained a defeat without a war . . . And do not suppose that this is the end. This is only the beginning of the reckoning.'

14 September 1938, Con, *Daily Sketch*

The courtship – Adolf's way

The BBC gave its support to Chamberlain's appeasement policy and did little to air alternative views. Conservative MP Harold Nicolson was even told not to refer to the Nazi occupation of Czechoslovakia in his weekly broadcast. Nicolson was later told that his script had been personally vetoed by the Foreign Secretary. In a secret internal memo written on 5 October 1938, radio news editor John Copeman accused BBC management of a conspiracy of silence.

11 October 1938, Harold Hodges, *Western Mail*

Muzzled

Hitler's A.R.P. idea

It was reported that Hitler had openly criticised Churchill, Cooper and Eden. 'If a Duff Cooper, Churchill or an Eden came to power in Great Britain instead of Mr. Chamberlain,' he commented, 'we know it would be the aim of these men to make war. They make no secret of it. That compels us to be watchful and to look after the protection of the Reich. I have decided to continue with increased energy the further construction of our fortifications in the west.'

11 October 1938, George Middleton, *Birmingham Gazette*

Cooper, Eden, Churchill

*Your intellectual barrage balloon won't
be able to stop the peace doves!*

When speaking at a Nazi demonstration at Weimar on
6 November, Hitler accused British politicians, specifically Churchill, of 'warmongering'. Churchill issued a swift
reply, with a letter published in *The Times* the next day. 'I
am surprised,' he commented, 'that the head of a great State
should set himself to attack British members of Parliament
who hold no official position . . . Herr Hitler is quite mistaken
in supposing that Mr Eden, Mr Duff Cooper, myself, and
leaders of the Liberal and Labour Parties, are warmongers . . .
Let this great man search his own heart and conscience before
he accuses anyone of being a warmonger.'

30 October 1938, Erich Schilling,
Simplicissimus **(Munich, Germany)**

Superseded

In his Reichstag speech on 6 November Hitler said that Churchill 'has stated that the present regime in Germany ought to be destroyed with the aid of forces within Germany who would gladly co-operate. If Mr Churchill had less to do with wretched traitors who are paid by foreign agencies, and had more to do with Germans, he would see how mad his talk is . . . As long as others only speak of disarmament whilst continuing to incite war, we do not believe them and think their only desire is to repeat 1918. In that case, my answer to Mr Churchill must be: That happens once only and it will not be repeated!'

8 November 1938, Cecil Orr, *Daily Record*

Balloon dance

Lloyd George criticised Chamberlain for the Munich Agreement, stating that he had 'surrendered on Czechoslovakia', and 'had given a free hand to the dictators because the Government had nobody equal to deal with two such astute and ruthless men as Hitler and Mussolini.' He was cheered on throughout by Churchill and Clement Attlee in the House of Commons.

10 November 1938, George Whitelaw, *Daily Herald*

Only a mirage

RIVAL BANDS

Speaking on 8 November in the Munich beer hall where he staged his first, ultimately unsuccessful, coup d'état in 1923, Hitler stated: 'I have to warn Germany that I see a war campaign being enacted against her ... In England and France today there are men at the helm who desire peace, but there are others outside the Government who want war against us. It is that that I have to take into account because, according to their constitution, Churchill could become Prime Minister of Great Britain tomorrow.'

The cartoon is the first reference to Churchill's 'wilderness years'.

10 November 1938, George Middleton, *Birmingham Gazette*

A week after *Kristallnacht*, the deadly anti-Jewish violence perpetrated by Nazis throughout Germany, Churchill called on his fellow Conservative backbench MPs to join him in supporting a Liberal amendment to form a Ministry of Supply. He said that such a vote would make the Government act and 'make a forward movement of real energy'. His call failed. Only two MPs went into the Lobby with him. Churchill later wrote to Duff Cooper: 'Chamberlain has now got away with everything ... there is to be no real, earnest, new effort to arm the nation. Even the breathing space, purchased at hideous cost, is to be wasted.'

16 November 1938, Wyndham Robinson, *Star*

The gatecrasher

Winston: No! I don't want to get in. Only to open the door.

After the fall of Czechoslovakia, the likelihood of war increased along with Churchill's popularity, and many called for him to be appointed to the Cabinet. Chamberlain finally agreed to establish a Ministry of Supply but appointed the Minister of Transport, Leslie Burgin, to the post. The *Daily Mail* wrote that Churchill would have been a more popular choice, but claimed that he did not want the job. The *Evening News* said that Churchill should be appointed to the Admiralty or as Secretary of State for Air. The editor of the *Sunday Pictorial* wrote to Churchill to tell him that 'only 73 out of the growing total of 2,400 letters are against you joining the Cabinet'.

20 April 1939, George Middleton, *Birmingham Gazette*

'Bring him back — it's your last chance.'

According to the *Sunday Pictorial*: 'Each time the nation hoped Mr Churchill would
be called in to help, the nation was disappointed . . . Churchill, more than any
other politician, foretold the crises that Germany's re-armament would inflame . . .
While there gathers sullenly the hurricane that threatens to wreck our generation,
this one man who could stem the dark forces, this one man whom Hitler fears, is
thrust into the background and forced to endure a political impotence which is as
shameful as it is premature.'

23 April 1939, Thomas Arthur Challen (Tac), *Sunday Pictorial*

NEV.—'This Russian Pact must be a good thing. Everyone's on it!'

In March, Stalin proposed an alliance between Britain and the Soviet Union to enforce collective security and prevent German aggression. Chamberlain, however, was anxious about the idea of forming opposing blocs. France and Russia were already linked by a pact of mutual assistance, and ties between the Axis nations of Germany, Italy and Japan were strengthening. Churchill was very much for the military alliance and in the Commons on 19 May stated: 'I have been quite unable to understand what is the objection to making an agreement with Russia . . . It is like setting up an armoured umbrella under which other countries will be invited to take shelter as and when they seek to do so.'

24 May 1939, George Whitelaw, *Daily Herald*

Influential persons are strongly urging Mr. Chamberlain to bring Mr. Winston Churchill into the Cabinet so that Herr Hitler may be convinced of British determination.

Following Hitler's invasion of the remnants of Czechoslovakia, there was an awakening that the country should unite and, if not too late, bring Hitler's aggressions to an end. There were also calls in the press for Churchill's inclusion in the Government. He was no longer seen as a warmonger, but as a defender of democracy. By this time, although Britain had pledged to support Polish independence, Hitler's demands for Polish territory, including Danzig and the 'Polish Corridor', were intensifying.

5 July 1939, George Middleton, *Birmingham Gazette*

According to the *Star*: 'Prominent supporters of the Government in Parliament and in the country are urging the Prime Minister to find offices for Mr Churchill and Mr Eden. At the moment, the Prime Minister is resisting this pressure . . . Their appointment, it is held by their friends, would also be a guarantee that Britain meant business in the fulfilment of her European pledges. Its significance would not be lost on Germany.'

5 July 1939, Wyndham Robinson, *Star*

Cabinet reconstructions

According to the *Daily Worker*: 'No one trusts the Chamberlain Government. It is utterly and totally discredited. Therefore, they are looking for some way to boost their credit. They are thinking about putting in Winston Churchill. Not as one of a united anti-Chamberlain Cabinet, but as a "show piece" of a Cabinet still headed by Chamberlain himself. They consider he would do the trick with the public. Why should Churchill do the trick with the public? Solely because Churchill is associated in the public mind with opposition to the policy of collaboration with the Fascist dictators. Because the public feels that Churchill is the outstanding opponent of the "Munich policy".'

5 July 1939, Jimmy Friell (Gabriel), *Daily Worker*

Still on the doorstep

The day this cartoon appeared in the paper, Anthony Eden wrote to Churchill, saying: 'Low portrays us together on the step tonight.'

5 July 1939, David Low, *Evening Standard*

It was rumoured that the First Lord of the Admiralty, Earl Stanhope, and Viscount Runciman, Lord President of the Council, both supporters of appeasement, were about to be dropped from the Cabinet and replaced by Churchill and Eden. Public opinion of Churchill was now so fervent that on 13 July a Liberal candidate won a by-election in North Cornwall on a 'Bring Back Churchill' platform.

15 July 1939, Kimon Evan Marengo (Kem), *John Bull*

Off for the holidays

Opposition objects to adjournment of Parliament. – London News Item

Chamberlain announced that Parliament was to be adjourned for summer recess from 4 August until 3 October. Churchill, along with more than thirty other Conservatives, protested vehemently against such a long break, saying: 'It would be pathetic, it would be shameful for the House of Commons to write itself off . . . or reduce whatever strength it can offer to the firm front which the nation will make against aggression.'

The South African cartoonist quite clearly saw Churchill as the main symbol of opposition to the Government at this time.

7 August 1939, Bob Connolly, *Rand Daily Mail* **(Johannesburg, South Africa)**

H.M.S. Cabinet

In the War Cabinet Mr. Winston Churchill replaces Earl Stanhope as First Lord of the Admiralty, the position he held at the outbreak of war in 1914.

On 23 August, Russia and Germany signed the Molotov–Ribbentrop non-aggression pact, paving the way for the Nazi invasion of Poland. On 25 August, Britain signed an official Treaty of Alliance with Poland. Nevertheless, on 1 September Hitler's armies invaded Polish territory. By 3 September, Britain was at war and, on the same day, Chamberlain brought Churchill into the Cabinet as First Lord of the Admiralty. The Board of the Admiralty then sent out a signal to the entire British Fleet: 'Winston is back!'

4 September 1939, Talbot Ellison, *Birmingham Mail*

Trying to calm the seize

An American cargo ship, the SS *City of Flint*, which was carrying machinery and food to Liverpool, was seized by a German battleship on 9 October. The German crew declared the cargo as contraband and claimed the ship as a prize of war. The previous month, the German Propaganda Minister, Joseph Goebbels, had falsely accused Churchill of ordering the sinking of the British passenger liner SS *Athenia* in order to turn neutral countries against Germany. The *Athenia* was actually torpedoed by a U-boat off north-west Ireland on the first day of the war, killing ninety-eight passengers and nineteen crew.

25 October 1939, Harry Thackray (Thack), *Leeds Mercury*

A little innocent self-deception

In October, Churchill gave his first wartime radio broadcast in which he said that the Royal Navy were on the offensive against German U-boats, 'hunting them night and day . . . with zeal and not altogether without relish. And it looks tonight very much as if it is the U-boats who are feeling the weather, and not the Royal Navy . . . during the first month of the war we have captured by our efficient contraband control 150,000 tons more German merchandise – food, oil, minerals, and other commodities – for our own benefit that we have lost by all the U-boat sinkings put together.'

8 November 1939, Cecil Orr, *Daily Record*

Hitler's doubles go on strike!

On 8 November, a German carpenter, Georg Elser, attempted to assassinate Hitler in a Munich beer hall. The Berlin newspaper *12 Uhr Blatt*, falsely named Churchill as the originator of the attempted assassination, concluding: 'We, the German nation, are sitting in judgment on you Mr Churchill.' A 1939 book, *The Strange Death of Adolf Hitler*, alleged that the Nazis used four body doubles for Hitler, including the anonymous author, who also claimed that Hitler had died in 1938 and that he subsequently took his place. There was no evidence to support this.

12 November 1939, Peter Walmsley (Lees), *Sunday Graphic*

Language that he understands

Churchill gave another radio address reviewing the first weeks of the war on 12 November. He concluded by saying 'The whole world is against Hitler and Hitlerism . . . the final extinction of the baleful domination will pave the way to a broader solidarity of all men in all lands.' The *Leeds Mercury* called the broadcast an 'inspiring call to the nation'. But the German Foreign Office referred to it as a 'vulgar warmonger' speech. The *Hamburger Fremdenblatt* stated: 'The broadcast speech of the First Lord [of the Admiralty] contains a war programme which again confirms Britain's will to annihilation.'

14 November 1939, Harry Thackray (Thack), *Leeds Mercury*

'My b-beautiful b-b-bubbles!'

According to the *Daily Record*: 'Dr Goebbels is in a huff. Not only did Mr. Churchill not take the trouble to refute the ridiculous *Athenia* charges which have been levelled at him ceaselessly for weeks, but he omitted to make the slightest personal mention of the Doctor in the Sunday night broadcast … The fact that Mr. Churchill considers him beneath his notice has made the little Propaganda Minister squirm. Hitler, Goering and Ribbentrop got all the glory.'

14 November 1939, Harold Hodges, *Western Mail*

Heavy firing heard on the Western Front

Churchill's November address came as diplomatic and agents' reports revealed that the Germans were prepared to attack in the west. Churchill challenged Hitler to 'come and try to carry out his horrible threats against Britain'. 'The Allies,' he said 'were ready for him.' In response, Hitler, broadcasting from Munich, said: 'Germany never, never will capitulate … Britain does not want peace. We heard that again yesterday. I have already spoken in the Reichstag, and I have nothing to add. The rest will be said in language that Britain will understand. There can be only one victor, and that is us.'

17 November 1939, Rollin Kirby, *New York Post* (US)

Nightmare

After war was declared, the Admiralty announced a blockade of German trade and all contraband items, including food, animal feed, fuel and clothing, were confiscated. The measures, according to the *Daily Mail*, were 'to penalise Germany for her wanton and illegal methods of warfare, in which she has shown complete disregard for the safety of ships and human lives.' The strategy proved to be less effective during the first months of the war, as Germany was able to get many of its supplies from the Soviet Union.

24 November 1939, Cecil Orr, *Daily Record*

Winston: This is becoming a darned untidy war! (Two hundred mines have been washed up on the Yorkshire coast.)

According to the *Daily Mirror* on 25 November: 'More than 200 German mines have been washed ashore on the Yorkshire coast. One British minesweeper, in a single sweep, netted fifteen mines. The promised "intensified" sea war is on. "Neutrals would do well to cease trading with Britain altogether," it was said in Berlin yesterday, "and to divert their trade to Germany." There is no attempt in Germany to deny that mines are being strewn in the high seas, without regard to the rules of war.'

25 November 1939, Con, *Daily Sketch*

Salmon for breakfast!

The Battle of the River Plate, the first naval battle of the Second World War, was fought on 13 December 1939 in the South Atlantic. The German heavy cruiser *Admiral Graf Spee* had been sinking merchant ships regularly, but was tracked down off the coasts of Argentina and Uruguay by three British cruisers. In battle the *Graf Spee* was hit more than fifty times and was forced to take refuge in Uruguayan water. Four days later, incorrectly believing that the British had gathered a superior force to await their departure, the *Graf Spee*'s captain ordered her scuttled. It was a major victory for the Royal Navy. Churchill celebrated by saying: 'This brilliant sea fight takes its place in our naval annals and in a long, cold, dark winter it warmed the cockles of the British hearts.'

19 December 1939, George Whitelaw, *Daily Herald*

'Wish that man wouldn't keep spoiling my black-out.'

The scuttling of the *Graf Spee* was a severe embarrassment to the Nazi regime. In the German press, Goebbels falsely claimed the Battle of the River Plate as a victory, stating that the German battleship had sunk the three Royal Navy warships that had pursued her into Montevideo. Referring to these absurd claims, Churchill said he would be quite content to engage the entire German navy, using only the British vessels that the Nazis had falsely claimed they had destroyed.

20 December 1939, Cecil Orr, *Daily Record*

1940

The ubiquitous Winston: The evil machinations of the First Lord of the Admiralty.

According to the *Daily Sketch*: 'As everyone knows, the German hatred of our First Lord of the Admiralty, Mr Winston Churchill, has been expressed in various ways, which include many ludicrous propaganda stories. For instance, the Nazis pretend to believe that he sank the *Athenia* and arranged the Munich bomb attempt. Mr W. Heath Robinson has devised a series of brilliant and witty anti-Nazi exploits by the First Lord of the Admiralty, of which this is the third. It shows Mr Churchill making yet another attempt to blacken the fair name of the Nazis by electrocuting a Welsh Rabbit on the foothills of Mount Snowdon.'

10 January 1940, William Heath Robinson, *Daily Sketch*

'Come off the ice', cries Churchill. First Lord of the Admiralty, Mr. Churchill:
'Each neutral hopes that, if he feeds the crocodile enough, it will eat him last.'

In his fourth radio broadcast of the war, on 20 January, Churchill was scathing of the neutral nations, saying that they all hoped that the storm would pass 'before their turn comes to be devoured. But I fear – I fear greatly – the storm will not pass. It will rage and it will roar, ever more loudly, ever more widely . . . What would happen if all these neutral nations . . . were with one spontaneous impulse to do their duty in accordance with the Covenant of the League, and were to stand together with the British and French Empires against aggression and wrong?'

22 January 1940, Leslie Illingworth, *Daily Mail*

Fall in – and follow me

According to the *Daily Worker*: 'The peoples of the neutral countries are in revolt. For the first time since the outbreak of war they are openly and angrily denouncing the Chamberlain Government for its efforts to drag them into the war. The great flare-up of neutral opinion followed the brutal speech of Winston Churchill calling upon the neutrals to "do their duty" by getting into the war.' The governments of Norway, the Netherlands, Denmark and Switzerland had all protested over Churchill's radio address calling them to join the Allies. When told of this, Churchill responded: 'Asking me not to make a speech is like asking a centipede to get along and not put a foot on the ground.'

24 January 1940, Jimmy Friell (Gabriel), *Daily Worker*

The shockers shocked!

On 27 January, Churchill gave a stirring speech at the Free Trade Hall in Manchester in which he urged: 'This is no time for ease and comfort, it is the time to dare and endure. Come then: let us to the task, to the battle and the toil; each to our part, each to our station. Fill the armies, rule the air, pour out the munitions, strangle the U-boats, sweep the mines, plough the land, build the ships, guard the streets, succour the wounded, uplift the downcast, and honour the brave . . . There is not a week, nor a day, nor an hour to lose.'

29 January 1940, Harold Hodges, *Western Mail*

Adolf Hitler gave a speech at the Berlin Sportpalast on 30 January (the anniversary of his rise to power) in which he said: 'I must praise Mr Churchill. He frankly states what old Mr Chamberlain only thinks quietly to himself and hopes for secretly. He says: our goal is the dissolution, the destruction of Germany. Our goal is the extermination, if possible, of the German people . . . Evidently these gentlemen are of the conviction that we slept through these past five months. Since the day I stepped onto the political stage, I have never yet slept through a single day of importance, not to speak of five months.'

4 February 1940, Peter Walmsley (Lees), *Sunday Graphic*

The horse has other ideas!

Although it was reported in the *Daily News* that Chamberlain was 'firmly in the saddle', there were press reports and members of the opposition calling for a reconstruction of the Cabinet.

4 February 1940, Bill Baker (Pix), *Sunday Pictorial*

The sands are running out!

The first months of the war were dubbed the 'Bore War', later the 'Phoney War', due to the lack of military action on land. Both sides used this time to prepare their armies and air forces for an onslaught in the spring. In his speech on 27 January, Churchill indicated how important the additional months of preparation had been: 'Whatever may happen in the future, provided we do not relax our vigilance, Herr Hitler has lost his best chance. We do not wish indefinitely to continue merely awaiting the blows which are struck us. We hope that the day will come when we shall hand over that job to Herr Hitler, when he will be wondering where he is going to be struck next.'

11 February 1940, Wallace Coop (Wal), *News of the World*

Neutrality 'breeches'

The Altmark *incident constitutes a nasty kick in the Nazi pirates' pants.*

In February, the German tanker *Altmark* entered neutral Norwegian waters, carrying 299 British prisoners who had been picked up from ships sunk by the *Graf Spee* in the South Atlantic. HMS *Cossack* followed *Altmark* and on 16 February Churchill personally wrote the order to the Cossack's captain: 'You should board *Altmark*, liberate the prisoners and take possession of the ship.' In the ensuing fight, the *Altmark* ran aground and the British took control of the ship, releasing all prisoners and killing seven Germans. The incident greatly enhanced Churchill's reputation in the public eye.

19 February 1940, Arthur Potts (Spot), *Bristol Evening World*

'I've never been more insulted in my life!!'

Germany's war effort relied on imports of Swedish iron ore, which during the winter came from the port of Narvik, Norway. Churchill had long advocated for taking control of Narvik and the Swedish iron ore fields, but the plan was delayed due to Chamberlain's concerns about laying mines in neutral waters. It was, however, finally agreed that Operation Wilfred would go ahead on 8 April followed by a military landing at Narvik.

1 April 1940, W. H. Woodburn (Hengest),
Manchester Evening News

Confucius, he know

In a radio address on 31 March, Churchill said that the war was being prolonged by some nations maintaining neutrality, rather than fighting alongside the Allies. He said that 'many of the smaller states of Europe are terrorised by Nazi violence and brutality into supplying Germany with the materiel of modern war, and this fact may condemn the whole world to a prolonged ordeal with grievous, unmeasured consequences in many lands. Therefore, I cannot assure you that the war will be short and still less that it will be easy.'

2 April 1940, George Whitelaw, *Daily Herald*

Gulliver up-to-date

On 5 April, SS *Uhenfels* became the first captured Nazi vessel to be brought to port in London. On the declaration of war, the German cargo ship had been in the Indian Ocean. It made several attempts to return home, but in November 1939 it was intercepted and captured in the South Atlantic by HMS *Hereward*. Once brought to Britain, the ship was renamed *Empire Ability*.

3 April 1940, C. A. Munro, *Civil and Military Gazette* **(Lahore, India)**

Coming out on top

On 3 April, Chamberlain carried out a reshuffle of his war ministry. Churchill was made chairman of the Military Co-ordination Committee, which consisted of two other ministers and three chiefs of staff who would make strategic proposals to the War Cabinet. The public reacted enthusiastically to the move, including in America where Associated Press special correspondent DeWitt Mackenzie said that the appointment represented 'one of the most constructive moves towards victory which have been made for the Allied cause'.

5 April 1940, Fred O. Seibel, *Richmond Times-Dispatch* **(Virginia, US)**

Churchill, the 'Minister of War'!

Goebbels tried to persuade the German public, and the
neutral countries, that they faced increasing peril due
to Churchill's new role in the Cabinet. 'This is proof of
Britain's determination to intensify the war and conduct it
more ruthlessly against the neutrals,' declared an official in
Berlin. German newspaper headlines were in the same vein:
'Churchill's Dominating Cabinet Role' and 'Churchill's Task
is Extending the War', all indicated a fear of Churchill and
his more aggressive war policy.

**5 April 1940, artist unknown, *Berliner
Nachtausgabe* (Berlin, Germany)**

'Ugh – How we hate you!'

Churchill's new powers in the Military Co-ordination
Committee, as well as his increasing popularity at home,
meant that he became even more reviled in the German
press. 'Churchill's promotion to Supreme Minister of the
Armed Forces proves that the Imperialist Powers will make a
serious attempt to widen the theatre of war,' said the *Deutsche
Allgemeine Zeitung*. Berlin radio claimed that Churchill had
been elevated from 'warmonger to grand warmonger'.

**12 April 1940, W. H. Woodburn (Hengest),
*Manchester Evening News***

Bottled up

The Government's plan for a military landing at Narvik, Norway, had come too late. On 8 April, at the same time that the Royal Navy was laying mines, German forces landed on the Norwegian coast and the next day they invaded Narvik. Within 48 hours the Germans had occupied both Norway and Denmark. But by 13 April the Royal Navy had finally managed to clear the way to Narvik, sinking one German submarine and seven warships. The Admiralty announced that the port had been 'bottled up' by Anglo-French squadrons. According to the French Premier Paul Reynaud: 'The Nazi's North Sea windows have been closed. Not a ton of iron ore will leave Narvik for Germany.'

15 April 1940, Harold Hodges, *Western Mail*

'The Narvik sock!'

In addition to the counterattack at Narvik, there had also been successful British landings north and south of Trondheim and at three other points around Narvik. In the House of Commons on 11 April, Churchill brashly stated: 'The Norwegian batteries have had their successes, and I must consider the German Fleet crippled in important respects.' The cartoon compares Churchill to Popeye, the superhumanly strong sailor with his handy pipe.

16 April 1940, Stuart Peterson, *Sun* (Sydney, Australia)

The Royal Navy's success in Norway was not long lasting. Germany had many more men on the ground as well as air superiority. Deep snow and freezing temperatures hampered the Allied attempts at a counteroffensive. On 26 April, the British started to withdraw from Norway. Chamberlain's Cabinet came under severe criticism as a result. A group of senior MPs officially complained about the 'want of initiative' shown by the Government and some Conservatives started to press for a change of leadership. Churchill later wrote of the Norwegian failure: 'Considering the prominent part I played in these events . . . it was a marvel that I survived.'

3 May 1940, Leslie Illingworth, *Daily Mail*

Under fire

Following the Allied failure in Norway, the House of Commons held an open debate from 7–9 May. On the first day, Chamberlain tried unsuccessfully to justify the Norwegian campaign, but his arguments were frequently met with jeers. When he stood to speak, Leo Amery, former Conservative minister and Chamberlain's friend and colleague for two decades, evoked Cromwell's words to the Long Parliament in 1653 by saying: 'You have sat for too long for any good you have been doing. Depart, I say, and let us have done with you. In the name of God, go!' Harold Macmillan said that Amery's speech 'effectively destroyed the Chamberlain government'.

7 May 1940, Arthur Potts (Spot), *Bristol Evening World*

After Lord Chatfield resigned the post, it was rumoured that Churchill may be appointed Minister for Co-ordination of Defence, adding to his roster of political positions and influence over military decisions. In fact, the role ended up being made redundant with the functions of the office transferring to other departments. 'Meat needs mustard' was the advertising slogan of Colman's mustard at the time.

8 May 1940, Harold Hodges, *Western Mail*

Can we share your peace and quiet?

On the second day of what became known as the 'Norway Debate', Chamberlain was castigated by a number of high-ranking political figures. David Lloyd George called for his resignation and the Labour opposition turned the debate into a confidence vote on the Government. Despite being warned by Lloyd George that he should not become an 'air raid shelter to keep the splinters from hitting his colleagues', Churchill claimed full responsibility for the Norwegian campaign. The Maginot Line was a line of fortifications built by the French to deter a Nazi invasion. When the Germans invaded France on 10 May, they avoided the line altogether by attacking through Belgium and the Netherlands.

8 May 1940, Charles Werner, *Daily Oklahoman* (Oklahoma, US)

In London's toxic kitchen

Churchill: 'Do better, gentlemen, the appalling propaganda of 1914/18 must be surpassed by far!'

In his early radio addresses, Churchill rallied the nation against Hitler and his 'wicked men whose hands are stained with blood and soiled with corruption'. Goebbels, Hitler's Minister of Propaganda, in turn called Churchill 'the biggest and most experienced liar in modern history'. Britain had established the Ministry of Information at the beginning of the war to publish 'national propaganda'. According to historian David Welch, one of its tactics was to employ 'the notion of the barbarous Hun – first exploited on a massive scale in World War One – to show that they were still the "same aggressor"'. The man on the right of the cartoon is reading a book entitled 'Lives of Mass Murderers' by Max Ludwig (a German general from the First World War).

8 May 1940, Groth, *B.Z. Am Mittag* (Berlin, Germany)

Raiders passed

On 8 May, at the end of another stormy day of debate on the Norwegian failure, the House of Commons voted on a motion of no confidence in the Government. In a normal vote, the Government could expect a majority of more than 200 but this time Chamberlain secured a majority of only eighty-one. As the Prime Minister left the chamber, he was accompanied by cries of 'Go! Go! Go!' from across the House.

9 May 1940, Arthur Potts (Spot), *Bristol Evening World*

Chamberlain spent the next two days attempting to form a coalition government with the Labour and Liberal opposition. The leader of the Labour Party, Clement Attlee, confirmed that the party would be willing to join the Government, but not under Chamberlain. Labour would serve if another Conservative became Prime Minister. On 10 May, the day Germany invaded Belgium, the Netherlands, Luxembourg and France, Chamberlain went to Buckingham Palace to offer his resignation to the King and advised him to send for Churchill.

9 May 1940, Hal Coffman, *Fort Worth Star-Telegram* **(Texas, US)**

Taking over

'Mr. Churchill has expressed to me his strong desire that I should be a member of the War Cabinet, and I told him that I will gladly give him any assistance that I can in that capacity.' – Mr. Chamberlain in his broadcast last night.

Churchill was Prime Minister, but Chamberlain remained leader of the Conservative Party. As such, Churchill recognised the importance of having Chamberlain in his Cabinet. Churchill wrote to his predecessor to thank him for his promise of support, acknowledging that 'to a very large extent I am in your hands and I feel no fear of that'.

11 May 1940, Talbot Ellison, *Birmingham Mail*

SPITFIRE! . . . . The Lion gets a move on.

Churchill immediately formed a small, five-man War Cabinet, which included Chamberlain as Lord President of the Council, Attlee as Lord Privy Seal (and later as Deputy Prime Minister), Lord Halifax as Foreign Secretary and Arthur Greenwood as a minister without portfolio. Churchill also created and assumed the post of Minister of Defence. The wider Cabinet contained ministers from all parties including the Liberal leader Archibald Sinclair as Air Minister, in what Churchill liked to call a 'Grand Coalition'.

14 May 1940, George Middleton, *Birmingham Gazette*

For freedom

The Emergency Powers (Defence) Act, originally passed by Parliament at the start of the war, was extended on 22 May. The Act made 'provision for requiring persons to place themselves, their services and their property at the disposal of His Majesty ... or for maintaining supplies or services essential to the life of the community'. As Churchill told the American President, Franklin D. Roosevelt: 'Democracy has to prove that it can provide a granite foundation for war against tyranny.'

The popularisation of the thumbs-up signal is often attributed to Second World War pilots, and there is evidence that the Belgian army greeted British soldiers with the gesture as they made their way across the continent. In the early stages of the war, many monuments and statues were covered in sandbags to prevent bomb damage.

23 May 1940, W. H. Woodburn (Hengest),
Manchester Evening News

The new front door

After the swift and shocking German invasion of France, the news from the front line was increasingly worrying. Advancing units of the German army had driven a wedge between British and French forces in northern France and the British Army began its retreat to Dunkirk. Fearing that German attention would turn to the British Isles once the occupation of France was complete, the Government prepared for imminent invasion. On 27 May, General Ironside took charge of the defence plan for Britain. He focused on building a large scheme of coastal and inland defences, the purpose of which was to slow down an enemy invasion. Berlin Radio reported: 'General Ironside's new appointment proves that the people of London are beginning to understand what a grave turn the war has taken.'

28 May 1940, George Middleton, *Birmingham Gazette*

The window cleaner

'This rosy mist has taken a lot of getting off, but the job's nearly finished now.'

On 3 June, the evacuation of Dunkirk came to an end. About 340,000 British and French troops had been evacuated, but tens of thousands of soldiers had been killed during the retreat and a huge mass of military materiel was left behind. Churchill sought to temper the mood of national euphoria when he said in the Commons on 4 June: 'Our thankfulness at the escape of our Army and so many men . . . must not blind us to the fact that what has happened in France and Belgium is a colossal military disaster.' He warned of the possibility of invasion but said that he was confident in the nation's resolve to defend itself. Churchill ended his speech with the now iconic words: 'We shall fight on the beaches, we shall fight on the landing grounds, we shall fight in the fields and in the streets, we shall fight in the hills; we shall never surrender.'

6 June 1940, George Whitelaw, *Daily Herald*

'I will remain loyal to you for ever, Marianne!'

In only six weeks, German forces had defeated the French army and occupied most of France. Churchill summed up the seriousness of the situation in the Commons on 18 June when he said: 'The Battle of France is over. I suspect that the Battle of Britain is about to begin.' This German cartoon portrays an angry and distraught France, abandoned by the British at Dunkirk. More than 100,000 French troops had been rescued during Operation Dynamo, but thousands more were left behind on the beach and were forced to surrender to the Germans. Marianne is a symbolic figure of the French Republic, originating from the French Revolution. She represents the values of liberty, equality and fraternity.

4 July 1940, Carl Franz Bauer, *Fliegende Blätter* **(Munich, Germany)**

Keeping him to his word

On 22 June, an armistice was signed between France and Germany. The agreement said: 'The French war fleet is to collect in ports . . . under German and/or Italian control . . . The German Government solemnly declares to the French Government that it does not intend to use the French War Fleet for the purposes of the war.' But Churchill did not trust Hitler to honour this commitment. On 3 July, Churchill ordered the Royal Navy to sink the French fleet, which was at anchor in the port of Mers el-Kebir, Algeria. 'I have never in my experience seen so grim and sombre a question as to what we were to do about the French fleet discussed in the Cabinet,' Churchill said. 'The Cabinet took the decision to seize the French fleet with aching hearts but with unanimity.'

6 July 1940, George Middleton, *Birmingham Gazette*

At Number Ten

*'We shall defend every village, every town, and every city.
The vast mass of London itself, fought street by street, could
easily devour an entire hostile army, and we would rather
see London laid in ruins and ashes than that it should be
tamely and abjectly enslaved.'—The Premier's broadcast.*

From 10 July, the Royal Air Force and Royal Navy were called
on to defend the nation against large-scale attacks by the
Luftwaffe. The Battle of Britain had commenced. On 14 July,
Churchill addressed the public in a radio broadcast: 'And now
it has come to us to stand alone in the breach, and face the
worst that the tyrant's might and enmity can do . . . Be the
ordeal sharp or long or both, we shall seek no terms, we shall
tolerate no parley; we may show mercy – we shall ask for
none.' The speech became known as 'The War of the Unknown
Warriors' and was heard by nearly two-thirds of the British
adult population.

15 July 1940, Talbot Ellison, *Birmingham Mail*

When Father says turn in . . .

As air raids were taking place day and night, Churchill asked ministers to 'live on the job'. Whitehall became a dormitory as well as a place of work for hundreds of civil servants. Churchill lived in his private quarters above the Cabinet Room. A. V. Alexander, the new First Lord, lived at Admiralty House, while the Chief of the Imperial General Staff, Sir Edmund Ironside, had a bed in his office. It was reported that the War Office was just as busy during the night as in the daytime.

20 July 1940, George Middleton, *Birmingham Gazette*

The song of the wheels

Behind closed doors, there was grave concern about the slow delivery of American supplies and Britain's lack of preparedness should Germany invade. But Churchill was determined to keep the public morale high. In a speech he said, 'From the British point of view our military situation is now such that we are confident that we can beat off any form of attack. Our defences are ten times as strong as they were when the war began. Around our coasts we have well-armed men who proved themselves more than a match for the Nazi troops whenever they met face-to face-in Flanders. Our Navy is still the strongest in the world. Our Air Force is growing more rapidly than Hitler's.' Some good news came on 24 July, when an agreement was signed for the United States to supply more than 14,000 aircraft over the next two years.

26 July 1940, Jock Leyden, *Daily News* **(Durban, South Africa)**

Following the Dunkirk evacuation, the RAF had been reduced to only 520 battle-worthy aircraft. But during the early days of the Battle of Britain, aircraft production rose significantly under the direction of the newspaper magnate turned Minister of Aircraft Production, Lord Beaverbrook. British manufacturers managed to increase production to more than 500 fighters per month, more than double the number estimated by German intelligence. As a result, by September, Fighter Command had a fleet of some 1,400 aircraft.

9 August 1940, George Whitelaw, *Daily Herald*

And the game continues . . .

Benito Mussolini, the fascist leader of Italy, felt sure that a German victory was imminent after the occupation of France and so, on 10 June, Italy declared war on Britain and France. 'People who go to Italy to look at ruins,' Churchill prophesied, 'won't have to go as far as Naples and Pompeii in the future.' By August, the Luftwaffe had received orders to achieve air superiority by attacking RAF infrastructure and airfields. The German air force began a campaign of mass destruction on 13 August, but with only moderate success. On 15 August, for example, 100 German bombers attacked in the North-East, and 800 across the south of England. The RAF responded valiantly and, by the end of the day, seventy-six German aircraft had been shot down, with the loss of only eight British pilots.

21 August 1940, Benedito Carneiro Bastos Barreto (Belmonte), *Folha Da Manhã* (São Paulo, Brazil)

Cause – and effect

On 20 August, at the height of the Battle of Britain, Churchill gave a speech in the House of Commons in which he said: 'The gratitude of every home in our Island . . . goes out to the British airmen who, undaunted by odds, unwearied in their constant challenge and mortal danger, are turning the tide of world war by their prowess and by their devotion. Never in the field of human conflict was so much owed by so many to so few.' The *News Chronicle* stated: 'Each of Mr Churchill's war broadcasts are brilliant . . . he has the gift of putting on the air his own buoyant confidence and of giving an imaginative impulse to the national war effort.'

21 August 1940, George Whitelaw, *Daily Herald*

'*Confronted at the beginning of May with such a prospect . . .
few would have believed we could survive.*' – Mr Churchill

'*We few, we happy few, we band of brothers.*'

At a time of increasingly brutal warfare, the ongoing presence in the Government of Cabinet ministers who had supported disarmament or the signing of the Munich Agreement prompted attacks from both the Labour and Liberal Party. Fierce criticism came from the press and from an anonymously authored polemic, entitled Guilty Men, which attacked fifteen men deemed responsible for appeasement and for the failure to properly re-equip British forces. The subtitle was 'Let the guilty men retire' and it effectively destroyed the reputations of former prime ministers Stanley Baldwin and Neville Chamberlain.

22 August 1940, Jimmy Friell (Gabriel), *Daily Worker*

TOTAL WAR IN WHITEHALL

As part of a shake-up of government operations, Churchill asked all departments to 'cut the cackle' and use simple English to save reading time. He told officials that reports, often laden with what *The Times* called 'Whitehall jargon', had to be shorter and that the aim was to set out the main points in a series of brief, crisp paragraphs. 'Official jargon makes soul-destroying reading,' he said in the *Bradford Observer*, 'and time and temper will be saved if its place is taken by simple statements of fact.'

22 August 1940, Wyndham Robinson, *Star*

Ineffective 'Axis'

In his 'The Few' speech, Churchill said: 'One of the ways to bring this war to a speedy end is to convince the enemy, not by words but by deeds, that we have both the will and the means, not only to go on indefinitely but to strike heavy and unexpected blows.' His words made it clear that, although an invasion of Britain was still a real possibility, Churchill was also planning offensive action.

The oak tree is Britain's national tree and a symbol of strength. The oak, like Churchill, is closely associated with the Royal Navy, as all ships were made of oak until the mid-nineteenth century.

23 August 1940, Cecil Orr, *Daily Record*

Strength through joy

On 23 August, the Royal Air Force reached the milestone of having shot down 1,002 Luftwaffe aircraft since the Battle of Britain began. On 24 August, however, London was bombed in the first daytime raid on the city. Bombs landed on central London and parts of the East End were set ablaze. For each of the next twelve days, 600 German bombers attacked British cities and airfields.

25 August 1940, George Aria, *Sun* (Sydney, Australia)

—"I THINK HE MEANS IT THIS TIME, RIBBENTROP.."

In his speech on 20 August, Churchill had emphasised the 'solid grounds' for confidence in being able to defend the nation. 'The whole of the warring nations are engaged, not only soldiers, but the entire population, men, women, and children. The fronts are everywhere. The trenches are dug in the towns and streets. Every village is fortified. Every road is barred,' he said. The Home Guard, an armed citizen militia, had been established in May. During the summer of 1940, it helped man anti-aircraft guns and also guarded roadblocks and coastal areas.

31 August 1940, Kimon Evan Marengo (Kem), *Sunday Pictorial*

Pardon us if we make a few changes too

On 14 August, US President Franklin D. Roosevelt, without approval from Congress, agreed to provide the British with fifty destroyers. In return, Churchill allowed the US to lease British naval bases in Canada, Bermuda, the Bahamas and the West Indies, for ninety-nine years. Of the fifty destroyers, only nine were serviceable but the psychological importance of the agreement was immense; it committed America, to an extent not previously envisaged, to the assistance of Britain's war effort. It was a glimmer of hope at a time when the Axis powers had control of much of Europe and Italy was making gains in British-held African territory.

4 September 1940, Herbert Lawrence Block (Herblock),
Newspaper Enterprise Association **(Chicago, US)**

'Horatius of the skies'
Never was so much owed by so many to
so few. – The Prime Minister

By early September, German air raids were near daily and the losses heavy. In the week leading up to 5 September, fifty fighter pilots were killed along with more than 450 civilians, many of them workers in aircraft factories. Churchill chose to withhold the details of these heavy losses so as not to damage public morale.

The RAF roundel, the circular identification mark, was painted on all aircraft to distinguish them. Horatius was an officer in the Roman army who famously defended Rome from the invading Etruscans in the late sixth century BC.

4 September 1940, Clive Upton, *Daily Sketch*

Winston's 'air' raid

Churchill once again broadcast to the nation on 11 September. The Luftwaffe had changed tactics and was now concentrating its firepower against civilian populations in major cities. Churchill spoke of Hitler having '[kindled] a fire in British hearts, here and all over the world, which will glow long after all traces of the conflagration he has caused in London have been removed. He has lighted a fire which will burn with a steady and consuming flame until the last vestiges of Nazi tyranny have been burnt out.' In late August, the RAF started to retaliate by hitting commercial and industrial targets in Berlin.

12 September 1940, George Middleton, *Birmingham Gazette*

'Churchill's weather'

The British Government was still operating under the assumption that there would be a German invasion. In his speech on 11 September Churchill said: 'We must regard the next week or so as a very important period in our history. It ranks with the days when the Spanish Armada was approaching the Channel and Drake was finishing his game of bowls, or when Nelson stood between us and Napoleon's Grand Army at Boulogne . . . , Every man and woman will therefore prepare himself to do his duty . . .'

Throughout September, the RAF carried out a number of significant raids at Channel ports in German-occupied France and the Low Countries, sinking hundreds of German invasion barges.

22 September 1940, Peter Walmsley (Lees), *Sunday Graphic*

A match . . .

Roosevelt declared that there would be closer military, naval and air co-operation between America and Britain as a response to diplomatic pressure. This was echoed by Under Secretary of State Sumner Welles, who also renewed the pledge of full material support to Britain in its fight with the Nazis. According to an editorial in the *New York Herald Tribune*, there was 'a need for the United States and Britain to begin looking to the future constructively'. 'Churchill,' it said, had 'captured the imagination of the American public which had led them to renewing their faith in Britain'.

4 October 1940, Clive Upton, *Daily Sketch*

Unfriendly act

Japan warned Britain about reopening the Burma Road, which had earlier been used by Britain and the United States (when Burma was a British colony) to deliver supplies to China during the Second Sino-Japanese war. Having agreed with the Japanese that the road be closed for three months, it was due to reopen on 17 October. Churchill advised Japan that neither Britain nor the United States were accustomed to submitting to threats and said that he hoped the 'prudence and patience' that Japan had often shown would still prevail.

9 October 1940, W. H. Woodburn (Hengest), *Manchester Evening News*

Churchill had broadcast only infrequently before the war (he had fallen out with the BBC in the 1920s over its decision to broadcast statements from the leaders of the general strike) but recognised the importance of speaking directly to the nation during this time of national emergency. He would go on to make thirty-three radio speeches during the war. Meanwhile, a coup was staged in Romania in September that brought the Fascist-sympathising dictator, Ion Antonescu, to power. Romania would officially join the Axis coalition in November. Also in September, the Allies launched an attack on the port of Dakar, French West Africa, in an attempt to replace the local Vichy administration with a Free French government. The operation failed and the Allies were forced to withdraw.

9 October 1940, George Middleton, *Birmingham Gazette*

Forty-seven million Churchills can't be wrong

On 21 October, Churchill broadcast to the people of France, promising them that Britain wanted 'to beat the life and soul out of Hitler and Hitlerism'. He finished by saying: 'Good night, then; sleep to gather strength for the morning. For the morning will come. Brightly will it shine upon the brave and true . . . *Vive la France!*'

The American press welcomed the defiant speech as the utterance of a man confident of victory. The *New York Times* called Britain a nation of '47 million Churchills' because of its determination to resist the air bombardments and to stand against the Nazis.

23 October 1940, Will Mahony, *Daily Telegraph* **(Sydney, Australia)**

'That's a deal.'

The 1940 US election was dominated by the question of isolationism versus interventionism as war raged across the Atlantic. Roosevelt was running for an unprecedented third term, believing he was the only person fit to meet the Nazi threat. Voters were in favour of sending arms to Britain but also largely against entering the war. So when the Republican candidate Wendell Willkie warned that Roosevelt would drag the country into another war, the president was forced to promise that he would keep the country out of the conflict. Willkie was, however, very admiring of Churchill, praising him as a 'great and vigorous defender of democracy'.

4 November 1940, Clive Uptton, *Daily Sketch*

The passenger

The Taoiseach, Eamon De Valera, rejected Churchill's request to use Irish ports for the war effort. He stated that there could be no question of handing them over for British use while Ireland remained partitioned (as it had been since the Government of Ireland Act 1920). Churchill bemoaned the fact that the Irish ports had been returned to the Free State government in 1938: 'The fact that we cannot use the South and West Coasts of Ireland to refuel our flotillas and aircraft and thus protect the trade by which Ireland as well as Great Britain lives, is a most heavy and grievous burden.'

At this time, Ireland was still a member of the Commonwealth of Nations.

8 November 1940, George Middleton, *Birmingham Gazette*

If the lie gives him his boost, he has to shed baggage.

On 9 November, Neville Chamberlain died following a short illness. In the Commons, Churchill described him as possessing the most 'noble and benevolent instincts of the human heart – the love of peace, the toil for peace, the strife for peace, the pursuit of peace, even at great peril, and certainly to the utter disdain of popularity and clamour'. But, he added, Chamberlain had been 'deceived and cheated by a wicked man', referring to the false promises made by Hitler at Munich. Some MPs criticised Churchill's eulogy for its faint praise.

21 November 1940, Carl Franz Bauer,
Fliegende Blätter **(Munich, Germany)**

Following the signing of the Anglo-American destroyers-for-bases deal, Churchill predicted that the two nations had entered an age of greater collaboration. 'I do not view the process with any misgivings,' he said in 'The Few' speech of August 1940. 'I could not stop it if I wished; no one can stop it. Like the Mississippi, it just keeps rolling along.' The link between the two nations was about to become even stronger. In December Churchill warned Roosevelt that Britain could no longer pay for supplies, and, in response, Roosevelt proposed the Lend-Lease Act (signed in March 1941). The US would supply the Allies with more than $50 billion of food, oil and equipment to be paid for after the war. In a radio address broadcast at the end of 1940, Roosevelt said that he intended for America to become the 'arsenal of democracy'.

6 December 1940, Wyndham Robinson, *Star*

By October 1940 more than 500 British merchant ships had been sunk in the Atlantic. According to the *Bradford Observer* (28 February 1940), Churchill referred to U-boats as 'these rats of the sea', which were 'engaged in their cruel attacks on defenceless neutral ships, as well as on all branches of our naval and merchant services'. Due to the strain on food imports, the Minister of Food, Lord Woolton, cracked down on food hoarders, declaring: 'It is against the law to hoard, and if I find any hoarders I will deal with them remorselessly, ruthlessly and with intense pleasure.' On the U-boat menace he said, 'The German U-boat campaign has been out with all its force to starve us out, but we are still not starved out.'

12 December 1940, Leslie Illingworth, *Daily Mail*

That thrust is having its effect!

On the evening of 23 December, Churchill broadcast directly to the Italian people. 'One man and one man alone has ranged the Italian people in deadly struggle against the British Empire,' Churchill stated. 'After eighteen years of unbridled power he has led your country to the horrid verge of ruin . . . The people of Italy were never consulted . . . Surely the time has come when the Italian monarchy and people . . . should have a word to say upon these awe-inspiring issues.' According to the *Liverpool Echo*: 'The sound of the "Winston wedge" being driven in between Mussolini and the Italian nation was welcomed by millions.'

27 December 1940, Cecil Orr, *Daily Record*

'You've got the matches.'

At the end of the year, Churchill once again reviewed Britain's preparations to meet an invasion. He reassured listeners that 'the defence of the beaches is complete, from the north of Scotland right round the island. Enormous masses of machine-guns and fortified posts, with every device of defence, have been erected, and are guarded by large numbers of ardent and well-trained men.' Unbeknown to the British public, Hitler had ordered the invasion of Britain to be indefinitely postponed due to the failure of the Luftwaffe to achieve air superiority. His attention had now turned eastward.

30 December 1940, Clive Uptton, *Daily Sketch*

1941

Explaining it to Harry Hopkins

During negotiations for the Lend-Lease Act, President Roosevelt dispatched his personal representative, Harry Hopkins, to London to assess Britain's chances of survival. To convince him of the need for American support, Churchill took Hopkins to Dover to see the fortifications there and to look across the Channel at German-occupied France. In his report to Roosevelt, Hopkins wrote: 'Churchill is the Government in every sense of the word . . . I cannot emphasise too strongly that he is the one and only person over here with whom you need to have a full meeting of minds.'

Churchill was notorious for entertaining his dinner guests by re-enacting battles, particularly from his days in the Boer War, using table settings, cutlery, salt and pepper shakers, and toothpicks.

13 January 1941, David Low, *Evening Standard*

Nearly broke

Britain's arms expenditure for December 1940 and January and February 1941 amounted to $1 billion, but the nation's gold and dollar reserves had been so depleted that they came to only $574 million. The Lend-Lease Act was being worked out but, before it came into force in March, Roosevelt stipulated that all debts had to be paid in gold and by the sale of British assets in the US. Britain's ambassador to Washington, Lord Lothian, went public and told the American press: 'Well boys, Britain's broke.'

19 January 1941, Fred O. Seibel, *Richmond Times-Dispatch* **(Virginia, US)**

Promising youngster

As a result of the Emergency Powers Act, Ernest Bevin, the Minister of Labour and National Service, had complete control over the labour force and the allocation of manpower. By early 1941, Bevin introduced a series of wide-ranging laws that massively increased the number of civilians involved in the war effort. The Essential Worker Order, which became law in March 1941, tied workers to essential occupations and prevented employers from firing them without permission from the Ministry. From early 1941, it also became compulsory for women aged eighteen to sixty to register for war work.

1 February 1941, Cecil Orr, *Daily Record*

Let 'em all come

'We shall come through. We cannot tell you when, we cannot tell you how, but we shall come through. None of us has any doubts whatever,' said the Premier at Portsmouth.

This cartoon demonstrates that invasion was still very much at the forefront of the public consciousness but, in fact, the most senior members of government were already aware that any serious threat had passed. Cryptographers at Bletchley Park decrypted a radio signal sent by a German Enigma machine on 12 January. The message was an instruction to German wireless stations on the northern French coast (which would have been essential to co-ordinate an invasion) that they no longer needed to be manned after 10 January.

1 February 1941, Talbot Ellison, *Birmingham Mail*

Bluffkrieg!

Even though Hitler's attention had now turned towards the Soviet Union, Germany tried to keep up the appearance of an imminent invasion of Great Britain. Adapted invasion barges, for example, were still maintained at Continental Channel ports and training for an invasion continued into early 1941. Due to the decryption of the Enigma codes, however, the British Government knew that an invasion was not likely to happen soon and much of Germany's shipping was now moving eastwards.

2 February 1941, William Pidgeon (Wep), *Daily Telegraph* **(Sydney, Australia)**

'Give us the tools and we will finish the job.' – Churchill

Churchill's prediction that the UK and US would become increasingly linked was already coming to pass. Before Harry Hopkins left the UK, he concluded two deals: one for American aircraft carriers to transfer aircraft to Britain 'in case of urgent need', and another to allow for the sharing of British and American intelligence (including top-secret information that would give Britain an advantage over its enemies). In a broadcast to the nation on 9 February, Churchill said that his promise to Roosevelt would be: 'We shall not fail or falter; we shall not weaken or tire . . . Give us the tools, and we will finish the job.'

11 February 1941, Fred O. Seibel, *Richmond Times-Dispatch* (Virginia, US)

Churchill hangs up his warning

In his broadcast, Churchill declared that Britain had stood its ground, and the heroic efforts of the RAF and Royal Navy had prevented any attempt by the Axis powers to invade. But he also warned against 'overconfidence', and that Hitler may still 'be forced, by the strategic, economic and political stresses in Europe, to try to invade these Islands in the near future'. In such an event, he said: 'I put my faith in the simple unaffected resolve to conquer or die which will animate and inspire nearly four million Britons with serviceable weapons in their hands.'

11 February 1941, George Middleton, *Birmingham Gazette*

'Putting the wind in his sails.'

Churchill's 'Give Us the Tools' speech did its job and impressed the American press with its frankness and firm determination. The reaction was summed up by the *New York Times* comment section: 'Churchill need have no fear that his final plea will go unanswered. Americans will put their confidence in him and his countrymen; they will give them the tools to finish the job.' The *Sun* in New York stated: 'A good many thousands of fires in a good many thousands of furnaces in a good many thousands of American factories are already kindled so that, with all due speed, those tools may be forthcoming.'

12 February 1941, Clive Uptton, *Daily Sketch*

'Gentleman – in – the – audience obliges the professor!'

Following the Italian declaration of war in 1940, the British seized Fort Capuzzo in Libya (then under Italian colonial rule). Mussolini responded by launching an invasion of Egypt (which was under British military occupation). In December, the British Army's Western Desert Force, led by Lieutenant General Richard O'Connor, launched Operation Compass and struck back against fortified camps before pursuing the retreating Italian forces. In January, the port of Bardia was taken followed by the fortified port at Tobruk. In all, some 75,000 Italians were captured. On 7 February, the remnants of Mussolini's 10th Army surrendered at the Battle of Beda Fomm.

17 February 1941, Mick Armstrong,
Argus (Melbourne, Australia)

It will sink or float by your endeavours

In addition to the ongoing danger from U-boats, German surface warships (diverted from the invasion of Norway) were now also attacking merchant shipping. In January 1941, the German navy launched Operation Berlin in which the battleships Scharnhorst and Gneisenau raided shipping lanes, sinking or capturing twenty-two ships in two months. In response, the Royal Navy was forced to provide battleship escorts to merchant convoys. The Government also embarked on a shipbuilding programme to replace lost merchant vessels. In April, Churchill said in the Commons: 'We are building merchant ships upon a very considerable scale and to the utmost of our ability.'

HMS *Victory* was Lord Nelson's flagship at the Battle of Trafalgar.

24 February 1941, Clive Uptton, *Daily Sketch*

(In German and Italian): Winston – Wellington: 'I wish it were evening and the American destroyers were coming!'

By March, merchant convoys were under attack from U-boats, surface raiders and then the Luftwaffe, which contributed a number of long-range aircraft. One such model, the Focke-Wulf Fw 200 Condor, was said to be responsible for sinking more than 365,000 tons of Allied shipping between June 1940 and February 1941. On 1 March, Churchill told the Australian Prime Minister, Robert Menzies, that the sinking of merchant ships was 'the supreme menace' of the war. On 6 March, Churchill issued his 'Battle of the Atlantic directive', which gave the highest priority to defeating 'the attempt to strangle our food supplies and our connection to the United States'.

5 March 1941, Olaf Gulbransson,
Simplicissimus **(Munich, Germany)**

Into battle

Apart from the Battle of the Atlantic, British forces were fully stretched fighting the Axis powers in North Africa and, in March, some 60,000 British and Commonwealth troops were dispatched to the Balkans to assist the Greeks. The Italian army had invaded Greece in October 1940, only to be pushed back into Albania. On 6 April, the German army came to its ally's aid by invading northern Greece and launching an attack against Yugoslavia. Meanwhile, the pro-German Rashid Ali al-Gaylani, who had seized power in Iraq in early April, ordered his forces to attack the RAF base at Habbaniya, thus threatening Britain's oil supplies.

9 April 1941, W. H. Woodburn (Hengest), *Manchester Evening News*

Thumbs up!

In March and April, there was a sharp increase in the number of bombing raids over Britain and, on 9 April, it was officially announced that almost 30,000 civilians had been killed in air raids since the start of the war. On 12 April, Churchill visited the bombed-out ruins in Bristol, after one of the most savage and indiscriminate air raids yet launched upon the city. He shook hands with the public and told them: 'God bless you all. We will give it to them back.'

During the Blitz, Churchill became synonymous with the 'thumbs up' signal and was often captured on newsreel visiting factories or demolished cities and flashing his 'V for victory' sign or giving a thumbs up.

19 April 1941, George Finey, *Daily Telegraph* (Sydney, Australia)

Gladiator Games: 'Hail, Churchill. The victims salute you!'

Allied forces were in retreat on all fronts, much to the pleasure of this Italian cartoonist. Progress in North Africa had stalled as military resources were diverted to Greece. By the end of March, 60,000 tons of Allied merchant shipping were sunk in a single week and HMS *York* was destroyed in the Mediterranean. Then on 17 April, after eleven days of struggle, the Yugoslavian army surrendered to the Germans. The following day the Greek prime minister, Alexandros Koryzis, committed suicide. To rub salt into the wound, the cartoonist highlights Britain's military and diplomatic failures over the previous years.

20 April 1941, Giuseppe Russo (Girus),
Il Travaso delle idee **(Rome, Italy)**

The Axis-backed coup d'état in Iraq posed a threat to oil supplies, but also to the land bridge between British troops in India and Egypt, and to British power in the Middle East, which was essential for controlling the Suez Canal. On 17 April, British troops were flown into Basra supported by several divisions of the Indian army. In the subsequent months a campaign was launched by British forces that brought about the fall of Rashid Ali al-Gaylani's government, the occupation of Iraq and the increase of Allied power in the Middle East.

21 April 1941, Leslie Illingworth, *Daily Mail*

Churchill gave a report of the war in a broadcast on 27 April in which he sought to rally public morale. He opened by saying that he was aware of 'some uneasiness' on account of the 'gravity' of the war. But it was in the 'many painful scenes of havoc' in heavily bombed cities and ports that he 'found the morale most high and splendid . . . The British nation is stirred and moved as it never has been . . . This indeed is the grand, heroic period of our history and the light of glory shines on all.' He concluded that 'we naturally view with sorrow and anxiety much that is happening in Europe and in Africa . . . [but] we must not lose our sense of proportion and thus become discouraged or alarmed.'

28 April 1941, Wyndham Robinson, *Star*

Hitler's wasted shrapnel

During a speech at the Reichstag on 4 May, in which he recalled his so-called peace offers to Britain, Hitler launched into a tirade against Churchill, whom he claimed was 'behind this mad and devilish plan of starting war at any price'. Referring to Churchill as a 'bloody dilettante' and a 'madman running around Europe for almost five years to find anything that would burn', Hitler promised that he was 'determined to throw back for every bomb a hundred, if necessary, until the British people get rid of this criminal and his methods'.

6 May 1941, George Middleton, *Birmingham Gazette*

'No, Sir, we won't let it become a Herren pond!'

President Roosevelt gave a radio address from the White House on
27 May, in which he warned the American public that the war in
Europe had developed 'into a world war for world domination'. He
said that 'unless the advance of Hitlerism is forcibly checked now, the
Western Hemisphere will be within range of the Nazi weapons of
destruction'. Roosevelt announced the speeding up of the US shipbuilding programme and that his navy was increasing its patrols in the North
and South Atlantic to assist Britain. 'The delivery of needed supplies to
Britain is imperative,' Roosevelt declared. 'I say that this can be done; it
must be done; and it will be done.'

29 May 1941, Victor Weisz (Vicky), *News Chronicle*

Sister Anna, don't you see anything coming yet?

'Greece wrong! Crete wrong! Where is his help? Will he help me the way I helped others?'

On 24 May, the Battle of the Denmark Strait broke out between the British battlecruiser HMS *Hood* and battleship HMS *Prince of Wales* and Germany's *Bismarck* and *Prinz Eugen*. During the battle, the *Hood* (pictured in the cartoon) was destroyed with the loss of almost 1,500 men. The *Bismarck* also sustained heavy damage and was eventually chased down and sunk by the Royal Navy three days later. Meanwhile, by the beginning of June, Greece was occupied by Axis forces and British troops had been evacuated following the capture of Crete.

De Misthoorn was a virulently anti-Semitic magazine published in the Netherlands until September 1942.

7 June 1941, Claudius, *De Misthoorn* (Netherlands)

'Who? Me? Why I only wanted to keep the score!'

On 22 June, Germany invaded Russia. The Nazi plan, codenamed Operation Barbarossa, was designed to acquire oil reserves, agricultural resources and forced labourers, but the ultimate goal was to conquer the western Soviet Union and repopulate it with Germans. The invasion became the largest land offensive in history, with 3.8 million Axis soldiers crossing the border. In a hurriedly arranged broadcast that same day, Churchill said: 'No one has been a more consistent opponent of communism than I have . . . But all this fades away before the spectacle which is now unfolding.'

22 June 1941, Sidney Moon, *Sunday Dispatch*

The common cause

In spite of his personal feelings about communism, and the fact that the Soviet Union had signed the Molotov–Ribbentrop Pact that allowed Hitler to invade Eastern Europe in 1939, Churchill knew how to respond. In his broadcast he declared: 'Any man or state who fights against Nazism will have our aid . . . we shall give whatever help we can to Russia.' On 23 June, Churchill ordered intensified bombing raids on German bases in France to take pressure off the Eastern Front and, from 27 June, shared newly decrypted military intelligence with Stalin. 'If Hitler invaded Hell, I would make at least a favourable reference to the Devil in the House of Commons,' Churchill said.

24 June 1941, Will Mahony, *Daily Telegraph* (Sydney, Australia)

'Our new bedfellow.'

President Roosevelt responded to the German invasion of Russia by dispatching Harry Hopkins to Moscow to assess the Soviet military capability. The US War Department warned Roosevelt that the Russians would not last more than six weeks (a view shared by many members of the British Government), but Hopkins urged Roosevelt to provide assistance. The president agreed to extend the Lend-Lease Act to the Soviet Union, which allowed American-built weapons and supplies to be sent to the Eastern Front.

29 June 1941, Cy Hungerford, *Pittsburgh Post-Gazette* **(Philadelphia, US)**

International anthem

On Sunday evenings the BBC broadcast a radio show called *The National Anthems of the Allies*. After the Germans invaded the Soviet Union, it was speculated that 'The Internationale', which had been the Russian national anthem since the Communist revolution, would be included. But Churchill, a staunch opponent of communism, gave instructions that on no account was it to be played.

17 July 1941, W. H. Woodburn (Hengest), *Manchester Evening News*

Soviet war needs

On 15 August, Roosevelt and Churchill issued a joint message to Stalin proposing that a conference be held in Moscow to organise the supply and distribution of war materiel. The message assured that, 'We are at the moment cooperating to provide you with the very maximum of supplies that you most urgently need . . . We realise fully how vitally important to the defeat of Hitlerism is the brave and steadfast resistance of the Soviet Union and we feel therefore that we must not in any circumstances fail to act quickly and immediately in this matter on planning the program for the future allocation of our joint resources.'

16 August 1941, Talbot Ellison, *Birmingham Mail*

Churchill sailed on board HMS *Prince of Wales* to Placentia Bay, Newfoundland, for a secret meeting with Roosevelt on 11 August. The American newspapers reported that the president was on a fishing trip. The United States made five pledges during the talks, including to aid Russia on a 'gigantic scale', to provide a five-destroyer escort for every merchant convoy crossing the Atlantic, and to patrol shipping lanes as far east as Iceland. Two important agreements were also reached: first, to 'respect the rights of all peoples to choose the form of government under which they live'; and second, to ask Japan to cease any further encroachment in the South Pacific.

**17 August 1941, Bob Connolly, *Rand Daily Mail*
(Johannesburg, South Africa)**

The new air problem

Following these assurances from the US and the opening of a new, more distant front, Churchill returned to an atmosphere of over-optimism among the British public. The *Spectator* warned its readers: 'The lull in operations in the west ... has psychological effects which must be strenuously resisted. We tend inevitably to assume that we are through the worst ... On the contrary, Hitler has not yet lost the war in Russia... We are only experiencing an interlude in the ordeal, not its end. That end will come only through sustained endurance and intensified effort in production.'

20 August 1941, Herbert Lawrence Block (Herblock), *Newspaper Enterprise Association* (Chicago, US)

Bullets of decency

On his return from his meeting with Roosevelt, Churchill broadcast to the nation on 24 August. He reported that he and Roosevelt had 'jointly pledged their countries to the final destruction of the Nazi tyranny'. He also gave an update on the situation in Russia. Churchill said that 'scores of thousands of executions in cold blood are being perpetrated by the German police ... Famine and pestilence have yet to follow in the bloody ruts of Hitler's tanks. We are in the presence of a crime without a name.' Yet, he claimed: 'For the first time Nazi blood has flowed in a fearful flood.' He ended by reassuring Russia and the defeated nations: 'Help is coming. Mighty forces are arming in your behalf. Have faith, have hope, deliverance is sure.'

26 August 1941, Rollin Kirby, *New York Post* (US)

Simple lesson

In November, there were early signs that Japan was preparing for war. Since early 1941, the US had been arming China and trying to negotiate an end to the Sino-Japanese war. At the same time, the Americans, British and Dutch had embargoed oil and other products from entering Japan to deter any attack on their Asian territories. On 10 November Churchill gave a speech in which he warned that, if Japan and the US went to war, Britain would declare war on Japan 'within the hour'. The Japanese army spokesman in Shanghai, Major Akiyama, responded that Churchill's speech was a 'regrettable challenge'.

12 November 1941, George Whitelaw, *Daily Herald*

The Riddle of the Sphinx (Part 2)

On 18 November, Allied forces launched Operation Crusader, a surprise attack on the Axis forces under Erwin Rommel. The operation aimed to bypass Rommel's troops on the Egyptian-Libyan frontier, liberate the besieged troops at Tobruk and reoccupy eastern Libya. Churchill told the Commons that, 'This offensive has been long and elaborately prepared, and we have waited for nearly five months in order that our Army should be well equipped with all those weapons which have made their mark in this new war.' 'The enemy', he said, 'were taken completely by surprise.'

23 November 1941, Sidney Moon, *Sunday Dispatch*

Fashion parade, 1942

'Women are already playing a great part in this war,' said Churchill in the Commons on 2 December, 'but they must play a still greater part . . . We have not the power at present . . . to require women to serve in the uniformed Auxiliary Forces of the Crown or Civil Defence. We propose to ask Parliament to confer that power upon us.' In December, the National Service Act was passed. This new power was only to be applied to single, childless women between twenty and thirty, who would be required to serve in one of the three main auxiliary services, the Women's Voluntary Service or the Women's Land Army.

4 December 1941, Victor Weisz (Vicky), *News Chronicle*

The haunted Churchill home: 'Damn whisky, I'm seeing double!'

King George V of Great Britain and Tsar Nicholas II of Russia were cousins and were known for looking uncannily similar. They had a close relationship but, when Nicholas was deposed by Bolshevik forces in 1917, King George refused his cousin asylum, believing it would lead to unrest in Britain. Nicholas and his family were later executed.

The implication of this German cartoon seems to be that ties between Britain and Russia would eventually lead to the downfall of both. Churchill is depicted reading a paper entitled 'Sympathy for the Soviets' and has an image of King George VI on his desk.

7 December 1941, Oskar Garvens,
Kladderadatsch **(Berlin, Germany)**

In his speech yesterday Hitler declared for the first time that not Mr. Churchill but Mr. Roosevelt bears the prime responsibility for 'inciting' Poland to reject Hitler's 'peace offers', and thereby starting the war.

On 7 December, Japan's navy launched a surprise attack on the American naval base at Pearl Harbor, Hawaii, killing 2,400 Americans and destroying or damaging eight battleships. There were also co-ordinated attacks on British Malaya and the Dutch East Indies. On 8 December, the United States declared war on Japan. In turn, Hitler declared war on the United States on 11 December. In his 88-minute speech to the Reichstag, Hitler disparaged Roosevelt and the whole 'Anglo-Saxon Jewish-capitalist world', for their policy of 'unrestricted world domination and dictatorship'.

12 December 1941, Talbot Ellison, *Birmingham Mail*

WINSTON "NOT GUILTY"

Now that the US had been brought into the war, Roosevelt telegraphed Churchill, saying: 'All of us are in the same boat . . . and it is a ship which will not and cannot be sunk.' Churchill replied that he was 'enormously relieved at the turn world events have taken'. On 22 December, Churchill flew to Washington to co-ordinate strategy. Among other agreements, senior representatives from both nations agreed that Europe and the Atlantic should remain the priority, and that defeating Germany was, above all else, 'still key to victory'.

24 December 1941, Vaughn Shoemaker,
Chicago Daily News (Illinois, US)

Some chicken!

Mr. Churchill told the Canadian Parliament that the French generals told their Prime Minister in the dark days of Dunkirk, 'In three weeks England will have her neck wrung like a chicken. Some chicken! Some neck!'

During his month-long trip to North America, Churchill addressed both the US House of Congress and the Canadian Parliament. To Congress, he expressed relief that the US had 'drawn the sword for freedom and cast away the scabbard'. To the Canadians, he summed up the staunchness of British resolve to win the war with the famous 'Some chicken, some neck' quote. On New Year's Day 1942, Churchill and Roosevelt agreed to a declaration, issued by the 'United Nations', those 26 nations either fighting against, or under occupation by, the Axis powers, expressing their determination to win the war against Germany and Japan.

31 December 1941, Talbot Ellison, *Birmingham Mail*

1942

'If you hit my Judas – I'll hit your Judas!'

Churchill's relationship with Charles de Gaulle (by now the leader of the Free French) had soured by early 1942. De Gaulle had come to believe that Britain was using the war to claim former French territories in the Middle East; Churchill believed De Gaulle was prioritising his goals above all else. In August 1941, De Gaulle belittled Churchill in an interview with the *Chicago Daily News*, after which Churchill forbade British authorities from co-operating with De Gaulle. François Darlan, the de facto head of the Vichy government, was disliked by Roosevelt, who tried to avoid becoming closely associated with any French faction during the war.

3 January 1942, Oskar Garvens, *Kladderadatsch* (Berlin, Germany)

Sure shield

Churchill returned from his North American conference to discover a political crisis at home. Amid questions about his authority in the wake of the Washington agreements, Churchill demanded a vote of confidence in the Commons, admitting that 'things have gone badly and worse is to come'. But, just as the vote was taking place, it was announced that the Japanese military was advancing rapidly across British Malaya towards Singapore. The defence of Malaya was handicapped by the agreement with the US to prioritise Europe, causing a severe shortage of men and materiel.

21 January 1942, W. H. Woodburn (Hengest),
Manchester Evening News

'Sing-a-pour!'

He loves the rhythm of the rain

During the three-day Commons debate on the vote of confidence, Churchill took responsibility for Britain's continuing military failures. 'We have had a great deal of bad news lately from the Far East,' he told the House, 'and I think it highly probable . . . that we shall have a great deal more . . . No one will pretend that disasters like these can occur without there having been faults and shortcomings.' Churchill's prediction of more bad news came true on the same day, 27 January, as Allied forces in Malaya began a retreat to Singapore.

27 January 1942, George Middleton, *Birmingham Gazette*

One-man-show

Some Conservative backbenchers believed Churchill had taken on too many official roles. During the vote of confidence debate some MPs expressed doubt that it was possible for any one man to be both Prime Minister and Minister of Defence, and that they felt Churchill was acting as a one-man government. According to the Australian *Daily Mirror*: 'Churchill could have shown himself to be the great statesman that we know him to be. Instead, he has adopted the dictatorial attitude that the House has to agree to what he wants, that he will tell the House what to agree to, and not ask it to agree.'

28 January 1942, Victor Weisz (Vicky), *News Chronicle*

Stout fellow!

Churchill won the vote of confidence by 464 to one. Only James Maxton (a pacifist and member of the left-wing Independent Labour Party) voted against the government. After the result was announced, members of both sides of the House stood waving and cheering wildly.

31 January 1942, William Summers, *Buffalo Evening News* **(New York, US)**

Southerly Buster

'Hey, shut that confounded door!'

On 22 January, the Australian Prime Minister, John Curtin, was told that the British were considering evacuating troops from Malaya and Singapore to reinforce their presence in Burma (also a British colony). Curtin, furious that the importance of Singapore to Australia was not considered, wrote to Churchill, stating: 'The evacuation of Singapore would be regarded here and elsewhere as an inexcusable betrayal'. Curtin later said that the fall of Singapore 'can only be described as Australia's Dunkirk'.

4 February 1942, Norman Lindsay, *Bulletin* **(Sydney, Australia)**

After a week of fighting, General Percival surrendered Singapore to the Japanese on 15 February. In his broadcast that night, Churchill told the nation: 'Here is the moment to display that calm and poise, combined with grim determination, which not so long ago brought us out of the very jaws of death . . . Let us move forward steadfastly together into the storm.'

That same month, Churchill had bowed to political pressure and reshuffled his War Cabinet. Clement Attlee became Deputy Prime Minister and Sir Stafford Cripps took over as Leader of the House of Commons to reduce Churchill's responsibilities. The cartoon imitates 'All behind you Winston', the cartoon created by David Low after Churchill was installed as Prime Minister in May 1940.

22 February 1942, Clive Uptton, *Daily Sketch*

So wait for it!

Churchill called the fall of Singapore 'the largest capitulation in British history'. Moreover, the occupation of Malaya opened the door for further Japanese expansion. On 5 March, British officials gave orders for Rangoon – the capital of Burma – to be evacuated. Three days later the Dutch forces on Java surrendered. In his broadcast on 15 February, Churchill promised that this increasing threat would be met with 'dignity and renewed accession of strength'.

23 February 1942, Harold Hodges, *Western Mail*

'May I come in?'

After the fall of Burma, India prepared for a possible invasion by the Japanese and evacuated homes along its eastern borders. The emergency coincided with a visit to India by Generalissimo Chiang Kai-shek, the supreme commander of Allied forces in China. During the visit Chiang called on Britain to 'give real political authority to the Indian people ... India's participation in this war is striving for the victory of the democratic camp against aggression, but it also is vitally related to the liberty of India herself.' The question of Indian independence became an issue of global significance later in the year when the Indian National Congress launched the Quit India movement; it refused to co-operate with the British government or the war effort until independence was granted.

24 February 1942, George Whitelaw, *Daily Herald*

American bar
'Don't be sad, chubby chops. Let's drink
to your last bases of support!'

The cartoon shows Churchill on his recent trip to America being poured a large whisky by Eleanor Roosevelt so as to drown his sorrows over Britain's recent military setbacks in Asia and North Africa. German cartoonists regularly portrayed Churchill as a fat, inebriated buffoon with a drunk's red nose And Hitler often referred to him as being 'whisky-besotted' to undermine his leadership.

25 February 1942, Karl Arnold,
Simplicissimus (Munich, Germany)

With Churchill's permission, Britain's Ambassador to the United States, Lord Halifax, disclosed to Americans how British war production had increased by March. 'We are turning out twice as many tanks today as we did in August last year, three times as many as in February 1941 and five times as many as in July and August 1940. This year the production of light tanks will represent seven times the output reached at the end of 1941.'

5 April 1942, Sidney Moon, *Sunday Dispatch*

A chip off the old block

The Allied base in Malta, a British Crown Colony, was of vital strategic importance during the North African campaign as it served as a base from which to attack Axis supply routes to Libya and to resupply British forces in Egypt. From 1940 Malta had been subject to relentless bombing raids, but in early 1942 these air raids intensified. Between 20 March and 28 April, the Germans dropped 6,557 tons of bombs on the island. The RAF and land defences held out, but with significant losses of men and materiel. On 15 April, King George VI awarded the George Cross to the people of Malta 'to bear witness to the heroism and devotion of its people'. The George Cross remains on the flag of Malta to this day.

13 April 1942, Sam Wells, *Herald* (Melbourne, Australia)

'I trust that no mother will ever have cause to weep in consequence of any actions of mine.' – Hitler, September 8, 1938

In a broadcast on 10 May, Churchill told the nation that the Soviet government had expressed fear that the Germans would use poison gas against the Russian people. Churchill explained that the British would 'treat the unprovoked use of poison gas against our Russian ally exactly as if it were used against ourselves . . . [we will] carry gas warfare on the largest possible scale far and wide against military objectives in Germany. It is thus for Hitler to choose whether he wishes to add this additional horror to aerial warfare.' The German press, however, reported that Churchill, 'mad with desperation', had been the first to threaten use of chemical weapons.

12 May 1942, Victor Weisz (Vicky), *News Chronicle*

Stupid August and his Clown. 'He thinks I'm mending it, but I'm cutting out the best bits for him!'

Another common theme among German cartoonists was to show the United States exploiting Britain's weaknesses. There was some truth to this idea. After the fall of Singapore, the Australian government no longer trusted Churchill to defend its territory. Henceforth, Australian Prime Minister John Curtin noted in December 1941, 'Australia looks to America, free of any pangs as to our traditional links or kinship with the United Kingdom'. In March, the Cripps Mission, a British delegation sent to secure full Indian co-operation in the war effort, failed. Also in March, the US agreed, on Churchill's request, to send troops to New Zealand to defend it against a Japanese invasion. The British Empire's position in global politics was beginning to be supplanted by the United States.

'August' is possibly a reference to Emperor Augustus, founder of the Roman Empire.

15 May 1942, Reinhard Beuthien,
Lustige Blätter (**Berlin, Germany**)

Witchcraft at the Carlton Club

The Conservative MP for Kidderminster, Sir John Wardlaw-Milne, criticised Churchill in the Commons on 19 May for all the military failures that had taken place in recent years amid loud cheers in the chamber. He accused the Government of being 'puppets of the Prime Minister' and added 'What are the Government? One man.' In July, Wardlaw-Milne would try to force Churchill out by tabling a motion of no confidence.

The Carlton Club was the original home of the Conservative Party. It was at the club that the 1922 Committee, a group of backbench MPs that presents the views of the rank-and-file members to the party leader, was founded.

21 May 1942, W. H. Woodburn (Hengest),
Manchester Evening News

In his broadcast on 10 May Churchill said: 'We are urged from many quarters to invade the continent of Europe and so form a second front.' He welcomed this 'militant, aggressive spirit of the British nation . . . Is it not far better that in the thirty-second month of this hard war we should find this general desire to come to the closest grips with the enemy than that there should be any signs of war weariness.' In May, Britain and Russia had signed a mutual assistance agreement formalising their military and political alliance. But, despite Stalin's requests, there was to be no second front in Europe that year due to a lack of American troops and equipment.

3 June 1942, John McCutcheon, *Chicago Tribune* (Illinois, US)

With the war being fought on so many fronts, Churchill crossed the Atlantic for seven days of talks with Roosevelt to co-ordinate strategy. The two leaders discussed the opening up of a second front in Europe but decided, instead, to begin preparations for a joint invasion of the North African colonies of Vichy France. To facilitate this plan, Roosevelt appointed General Dwight D. Eisenhower to the post of Commander-in-Chief of US Forces in the European Theatre of Operations.

The previous month, Major League Baseball had committed to financially supporting the war effort by donating receipts from games. Special charity drives and war bond games were also held to encourage Americans to donate to the war effort. Over the course of the war, over 85 million Americans purchased war bonds, totalling approximately $185 billion.

22 June 1942, Ross A. Lewis, *Milwaukee Journal* (Wisconsin, US)

Second front

On 21 June, the Axis forces captured the port of Tobruk, Libya – which was of great strategic value due its deep-water port – and took more than 30,000 Allied prisoners. The defeat also allowed Axis forces under Rommel to advance towards Egypt. Churchill later wrote of the incident: 'Defeat is one thing; disgrace is another.' The incident prompted a surge of resentment across Britain. Churchill's critics forced a vote of censure against him in the House of Commons. Churchill won the vote easily, but the Labour MP Aneurin Bevan reflected a widespread feeling when he declared: 'The Prime Minister wins debate after debate and loses battle after battle.'

25 June 1942, Herbert Lawrence Block (Herblock),
Newspaper Enterprise Association **(Chicago, US)**

The Winston touch

Mr. Churchill, whose absence in America is holding up his reply to his critics, is stated to have said that there is no danger of losing Egypt.

Churchill was staying in the White House when he learned of the capture of Tobruk. He returned to London on 25 June to what he called 'a beautiful row'. The debate on the vote of censure began on 1 July – on the same day Churchill learned that Rommel had reached El Alamein in Egypt, 200 miles from Cairo.

27 June 1942, George Middleton, *Birmingham Gazette*

Churchill returned to the Commons in a fighting mood to answer his critics. On the second day of the debate, he said: 'Everything that could be thought of or raked up has been used to weaken confidence in the Government ... to represent the Government as a set of nonentities over whom the Prime Minister towers, and then to undermine him in his own heart and, if possible, before the eyes of the nation. All this poured out by cables and radio to all parts of the world, to the distress of all our friends and to the delight of all our foes ... If democracy and Parliamentary institutions are to triumph in this war, it is absolutely necessary that Governments resting upon them shall be able to act and dare, that the servants of the Crown shall not be harassed by nagging and snarling, that enemy propaganda shall not be fed needlessly out of our own hands ... I am your servant, and you have the right to dismiss me when you please. What you have no right to do is to ask me to bear responsibilities without the power of effective action.'

1 July 1942, W. H. Woodburn (Hengest), *Manchester Evening News*

Who will betray whom?

In May, Vyacheslav Molotov, the Soviet Minister of Foreign Affairs (depicted here with the moustache), had visited Britain to sign the agreement of mutual assistance. Molotov then continued across the Atlantic to meet Roosevelt. Molotov's aim in both meetings had been to convince the respective leaders to invade France and ease the pressure on the Eastern Front. Both Churchill and Roosevelt were coy about their ability to do so in the next year. They were fighting wars in the Pacific, Middle East and North Africa, and it was potentially beneficial to them to have a large portion of German forces tied up in Russia.

Here, the German cartoonist attempts to highlight the animosities and hostility that may still have existed between Britain and the Soviet Union. On the left, Molotov is being made to sign a treaty entitled 'Soviet Russia renounces Europe' and, on the right, Churchill is made to sign the 'Secret Treaty' entitled 'England renounces Europe'.

24 July 1942, Balkie, *Lustige Blätter* (Berlin, Germany)

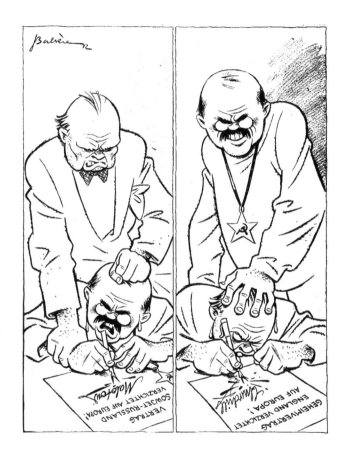

That's the way the wind blows

The mutual assistance agreement that had been signed by Molotov and Foreign Secretary Anthony Eden committed both nations to not seek a separate peace agreement with Germany. Furthermore, on 12 August, Churchill arrived in Moscow to meet Stalin for the first time – alongside Roosevelt's representative, Averell Harriman – to cement the ties between the nations. Though the two leaders did not seem to get along well personally and disagreed about the opening of a second front, the meeting, Stalin remarked, was 'of very great value'.

19 August 1942, Clive Uptton, *Daily Sketch*

On his way to Moscow, Churchill had stopped off in Egypt to discuss plans for a new North African offensive (which was to become Operation Torch). While there he travelled to El Alamein to inspect the positions on the desert front. The soldiers had been warned to stand by for a visit from 'Mr Bullfinch', the codename Churchill was travelling under. There was much speculation as to who Mr Bullfinch was, but when a figure appeared at brigade headquarters puffing on a cigar and flashing a 'V' sign, the troops shouted out: 'It's Winnie!'

23 August 1942, Sidney Moon, *Sunday Dispatch*

As now worn?

When Churchill flew to Moscow to advise Stalin that there would not be a second front in 1942, he said it felt like he was 'carrying a large lump of ice to the North Pole'. Despite Stalin's dismissive response, he did eventually endorse Churchill's alternative plan to invade North Africa and increase Allied bombing of Germany. Churchill's personal involvement was crucial in building an alliance with both Stalin and Roosevelt. This 'Grand Alliance', which he had helped forge – and which he had referred to in Moscow as a band of 'comrades and brothers' – now had a united strategy for defeating the Axis powers.

26 August 1942, George Whitelaw, *Daily Herald*

The big air cushion

Churchill arrived back in Britain on 24 August and arrived at Number 10 shortly before midnight. 'I am very glad to be back,' Churchill said as he posed for a photograph. When he was asked if he was tired, Churchill looked surprised at the question and shook his head. 'Tired?' he replied. 'Why should I be tired? I have been refreshed.'

26 August 1942, George Middleton, *Birmingham Gazette*

Handwriting on the pyramid!

On 28 August, cryptographers at Bletchley Park decoded messages that enabled the Allies to sink three Italian ships carrying fuel to Rommel's forces in Egypt. On learning this, Rommel launched a final attack on Allied forces in the Western Desert, fearing he would run out of fuel if he waited any longer. The decrypted signals also revealed where Rommel planned to attack and so the Allies, under Lieutenant-General Montgomery, deployed their artillery on Alam el Halfa Ridge. The ensuing battle was a major victory for the Allies. Rommel was never again able to launch a major attack.

1 September 1942, LeBaron Coakley, *Washington Post* (US)

"MY SPEECHES ARE GETTING WORSE"
—HITLER

ADOLF (AT BERLIN SPORTS PALACE 30ᵀᴴ SEPT 1942) HAD I IN FRONT OF ME A SERIOUS OPPONENT I COULD FIGURE OUT WHERE THE SECOND FRONT WOULD COME. BUT WITH THESE MILITARY IDIOTS ONE NEVER KNOWS WHERE THEY WILL ATTACK.

Churchill and his generals: Discussion of the issue of opening a second front

Hitler gave a speech in Berlin on 30 September in which he admitted that his rhetoric was 'becoming worse rather than better' due to lack of practice. He used the speech to lambast his enemies, calling them 'lunatics' and 'drunkards', but did express some anxiety about a second front, saying that 'when one faces military idiots, one cannot know where they will attack . . . For this reason, we must naturally be prepared everywhere.' On 19 August, Allied forces, most of them Canadian, had launched an attack at Dieppe as a test landing. The attack was a disaster; 60 per cent of the Allied contingent were killed, wounded or taken prisoner and only a few men reached their objective. Hitler crowed that the Allies had 'managed to hang on – one may say painfully – for nine hours, to be destroyed in the end'.

2 October 1942, J. C. Walker, *Western Mail*

During this period, Efimov regularly ridiculed Churchill's reluctance to open a second front in Europe as an example of British cowardice. The generals are labelled (from left to right): 'General Fighting-the-War-with-Someone Else's-Hands', 'General What-If-Something-Goes-Wrong', 'General Is-It-Worth-Risking', 'General Let-Us-Wait', 'General Let-Us-Not-Rush-This'. They are all depicted in the guise of Colonel Blimp, a pompous, ill-tempered, jingoistic character created by cartoonist David Low. When Low saw how his creation had been misused, he retaliated by drawing a cartoon of a Russian Blimp called Blimpski.

6 October 1942, Boris Efimov, *Pravda* (Moscow, Russia)

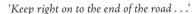

'Keep right on to the end of the road . . .'

There was mounting evidence that Germany was committing war crimes against the civilian populations of occupied countries, including expulsions, massacres and the execution of hostages. On 7 October, the British government proposed that a United Nations War Crimes Commission be set up, and President Roosevelt announced the same day that the US would support such a body. Churchill said that 'retribution for these crimes must henceforward take its place among the major purposes of the war'.

On 12 October, Churchill closed a speech in Edinburgh with lyrics from a Harry Lauder song: 'Keep right on to the end of the road,/ Keep right on to the end.'

14 October 1942, Victor Weisz (Vicky), *News Chronicle*

Safety first

The Prime Minister of South Africa, Field Marshal Jan Smuts, visited Britain in October to address both Houses of Parliament. Smuts said that the moment for a great Allied attack was approaching and that the defensive phase of the Allied strategy had now ended. 'Once the time has come to take the offensive and strike while the iron is hot,' he said, 'it would be folly to delay, to overprepare and perhaps miss our opportunity.'

It was reported that Smuts was in Britain for secret talks about the opening up of a second front in North Africa.

20 October 1942, J. C. Walker, *Western Mail*

The caddie

*Stalin: 'Yes, I admit that he has some very good shots,
but there is no doubt that I carry the greatest weight.'*

On 23 October, Allied forces under Montgomery launched an attack on the Axis forces at El Alamein in Egypt and advanced westwards. Progress was initially slow but, due to decoded signals that revealed enemy locations and shortages, the Allies made significant ground. On 27 October, as Rommel tried to organise a counter-offensive, the RAF dropped more than 80 tons of bombs over Axis positions in two hours. Meanwhile, the Soviets were bearing the brunt of German attacks on the Eastern Front. The Battle of Rzhev in summer 1942 had ended with 290,000 Russian casualties, earning it the nickname the 'Rzhev Meat Grinder'. German troops were advancing towards Stalingrad.

31 October 1942, Lino Palacio (Flax),
Cascabel **(Buenos Aires, Argentina)**

On 2 November, Rommel sent a signal to Hitler explaining that his forces at El Alamein were no longer capable of 'any effective opposition'. Due to a lack of vehicles and fuel, they could not even execute an 'orderly withdrawal'. The signal was decoded at Bletchley and Montgomery used the information to mount another attack. Within forty-eight hours, the Germans were in full retreat, leaving behind their Italian allies. Churchill joyously stated in his Mansion House speech on 10 November: 'We have victory – a remarkable and definite victory . . . The Germans have received that measure of fire and steel which they have so often meted out to others.'

8 November 1942, Sam Wells, *Daily Telegraph* (Sydney, Australia)

Between two fires

On 8 November, the Allies launched Operation Torch. Troops landed at three key ports in French North Africa – Casablanca, Algiers and Oran – with the aim of cutting off Rommel's retreat and securing North Africa. After fierce fighting, all ports were taken. On 10 November, the representative of the Vichy government, Admiral Darlan, concluded an armistice that confirmed the victory. There was also a successful Russian counter-offensive at Stalingrad on 19 November. Soviet forces launched a two-pronged attack that overran the Axis flanks and cut off occupied Stalingrad. As Churchill had promised, the North African campaign had helped by diverting aircraft from the east. Churchill was convinced that this period marked the turning point in the war. As he wrote later: 'Before Alamein we never had a victory. After Alamein we never had a defeat.'

22 November 1942, Alexander Saroukhan, *Akher Sa'a* (Cairo, Egypt)

'*Retribution is near.*' – *Churchill*

A year on from Japan having 'coldly, greedily and treacherously calculated' an attack on Britain's Far East possessions of Hong Kong and Malaya, Churchill sent a message to the people in Japanese-occupied territories. 'There will be no softness or respite for Japan,' he promised. 'Retribution was always sure. It is now growing near. Keep up your hearts we shall not fail you. For a year all our thoughts have gone out to you, Malays, Indians, Burmans, Chinese, Dutch and British who are suffering so cruelly.'

Hideki Tojo was the Prime Minister of Japan, and the main driving force behind the country's pre-emptive attacks in 1941.

9 December 1942, George Whitelaw, *Daily Herald*

Retort courteous

Asked yesterday who named the 'Churchill' tank, the Premier disclaimed personal responsibility, adding that no doubt the name 'afforded a motive to various persons to endeavour to cover it with slime.'

The Churchill Mk IV tanks were first used at Dieppe in August but were nearly put out of production due to their slow pace. This led Churchill to remark to Field Marshal Jan Smuts: 'That is the tank they named after me when they found out it was no damn good!' The tanks did, however, prove successful at the Second Battle of El Alamein due to their ability to take heavy fire. Churchill had been one of the first to promote the development of the tank during the First World War.

16 December 1942, Talbot Ellison, *Birmingham Mail*

Christmas roast

*'A foolish bird, Churchill! Too small for
two and just enough for one!'*

Roosevelt, through German eyes, is seen as gaining all the
military spoils to the detriment of the disgruntled and
self-entitled Churchill. Axis propaganda regularly portrayed
Churchill and Roosevelt at odds, constantly jostling for
power and pride. In fact, though the relationship had its ups
and downs, Churchill was determined to maintain close ties
between the two nations. The relationship between the USA
and Britain was, as Churchill told King George VI in 1942,
as though the nations were 'married after many months of
walking out'.

20 December 1942, Arthur Johnson,
***Kladderadatsch* (Berlin, Germany)**

'Who said I was the under-belly?'

Following the success in North Africa, Churchill became
convinced that mainland Europe could be attacked from the
Mediterranean via a full-scale invasion of Italy. He told the
Chiefs of Staff that their plans for 1943 should be rethought
to 'prepare the way for a very large-scale offensive on the
underbelly of the Axis'. (American General Mark W. Clark
would later refer to Italy as 'one tough gut'.) In his speech at
the Mansion House, Churchill said: 'Now this is not the end.
It is not even the beginning of the end. But it is, perhaps, the
end of the beginning.'

23 December 1942, Victor Weisz (Vicky), *News Chronicle*

1943

Two ways of looking at it

Although American public opinion supported immediate retribution against Japan after Pearl Harbor, Churchill and Roosevelt had agreed that war with Germany should be prioritised over action in the Pacific. Fearing that Australia was increasingly vulnerable, Australian Prime Minister John Curtin protested that the nation will 'refuse to accept the dictum that the Pacific struggle must be treated as a subordinate segment of the general conflict'. The statement, according to Roosevelt, 'smacked of panic'. In 1942 Japan had focused on invading Pacific island territory to isolate Australia and develop bases, but it suffered major defeats at the Battles of Midway and Guadalcanal. The Allies were also amassing forces in Australia and New Zealand for future counter-offensives, with 250,000 US troops in Australia by 1943.

3 January 1943, William Pidgeon (Wep), *Daily Telegraph* **(Sydney, Australia)**

'Believe me, Winston, the hat fits you perfectly. You just have to gradually get used to being led by me!'

On 12 January, Churchill and senior figures from the British military flew to Casablanca to meet with Roosevelt and the American Joint Chiefs of Staff. The main agreements reached during the conference were that action in the Mediterranean, in the form of the capture of Sicily, would be prioritised over a cross-Channel invasion that year. They also agreed that American troops, to the tune of 938,000 men, would be assembled in Britain to prepare for assault on northern France in 1944.

Berlin radio had reported that Churchill completely capitulated to Roosevelt at the conference, and cartoonists took delight in showing Churchill ceding control of the war effort.

13 January 1943, Olaf Gulbransson,
Simplicissimus **(Munich, Germany)**

Shadow over the Axis

At Casablanca, Churchill and Roosevelt called for the official recognition of Generals de Gaulle and Giraud as joint leaders of the Free French. The two made an agreement that they hoped to reach 'the liberation of France and the triumph of human liberties', with 'all French men fighting side by side with all their allies'. The British and Americans committed 'to use all our power, to make certain that no post-war government is set up in France except in accordance with the freely expressed wishes of the French people.' In reality, the relationship between De Gaulle and Giraud was frosty, and De Gaulle was still suspicious of the Allied leaders after they allowed Darlan, as a representative of the Vichy government, to retain control of North Africa following Operation Torch.

27 January 1943, George Whitelaw, *Daily Herald*

No deals with criminals

Roosevelt and Churchill further agreed at the Casablanca conference that Britain and the US would continue in the war until they had secured the 'unconditional surrender' of both Germany and Japan. In a press conference, Roosevelt explained that they meant 'no harm to the common people of the Axis nations', but they did intend to 'impose punishment and retribution upon their guilty, barbaric leaders'.

28 January 1943, Burt Thomas, *Detroit News* (US)

'Victory signs to you, Fritz – in Turkish.'

Turkey tried to maintain equal relations with both the Allied and Axis powers, but both sides put pressure on the Turks to join the war, or at least not side with the enemy. The Germans dispatched Ambassador Franz von Papen, who had successfully negotiated a treaty of friendship with Turkey in 1941 that prevented them from fighting with the Allies. Churchill then decided to travel to the Turkish town of Adana for a secret meeting on 30 January with Turkey's President İsmet İnönü. Churchill told İnönü that Turkey should 'play her part' only when 'circumstances were favourable' and the two agreed that British officers should fly to Ankara to make plans for 'the movement and subsequent maintenance of British forces into Turkey in the event of Turkey being drawn into the war'.

3 February 1943, W. H. Woodburn (Hengest),
Manchester Evening News

The eternal ventriloquist

On 2 February the frozen, starving and encircled German forces at Stalingrad surrendered, cementing one of the greatest Soviet victories of the war. After the German humiliation, Goebbels launched a propaganda campaign against 'Jewish Bolshevism'. Roosevelt and Churchill (who had now become ineffectual and subordinate to the Americans in German eyes) were 'to be presented as accomplices and toadies of Bolshevism, which is the most radical expression of the Jewish drive for world domination'.

In this cartoon, the Allied leaders are portrayed as puppets of the Jews. This was a constant theme of Nazi propaganda for the rest of the war.

7 February 1943, Oskar Garvens,
Kladderadatsch **(Berlin, Germany)**

Making it hot for him

On 11 February, Churchill reported on the events of the Casablanca conference to the House of Commons. He told MPs that the 'dominating aim' decided upon at the conference was to engage the enemy's forces 'on the largest possible scale and at the earliest possible moment'. They had also agreed to 'make the enemy burn and bleed in every way that is physically and reasonably possible, in the same way as he is being made to burn and bleed along the vast Russian front'. The result, Churchill reported, was: 'We have now a complete plan of action . . . For good or for ill, we know exactly what it is that we wish to do.'

12 February 1943, George Whitelaw, *Daily Herald*

There's something—

Following his speech in the Commons on 11 February, Churchill became seriously ill and was diagnosed with pneumonia. He continued to dictate letters with a fever of over 100 degrees but took over a month to recover. In a radio broadcast on 21 March, his first for a year, he began with a brief reference to his illness. 'Although for a week I had a fairly stiff dose of fever,' he said, 'which but for modern science might have had awkward consequences, I wish to make it clear that I never for a moment had to relinquish the responsible direction of affairs.'

(left) 17 March 1943, J. C. Walker, *Western Mail*
(right) **Mr. Churchill photographed on his way to the House of Commons for the first time since his illness.**
17 March 1943, *Lincolnshire Echo*

Churchill and Hitler both made speeches on 21 March. According to the *New York Times*: 'The world listened to two speeches yesterday . . . The contrast was striking. Through Churchill's speech rang the peals of victory bells. Here spoke a man supremely confident of success . . . who, therefore, calmly proceeds to map out a programme for a better world against the day "when the curse of Nazism has been swept from the face of the earth." The most that can be said about Hitler's speech is that it was staged to prove that Hitler was neither dead nor crazy, but all listeners seemed to agree that he looked and sounded shell-shocked, to say the least.'

22 March 1943, Victor Weisz (Vicky), *News Chronicle*

First order of the day!

Churchill's address to the nation contained his vision for a post-war Britain and plans for a fairer society in the aftermath of victory. He spoke of the need for a National Health Service and a fair education system to ensure that leaders could be drawn 'from every type of school'. During the broadcast, he was given a message from General Montgomery to say that the British Eighth Army was advancing against Axis forces in Tunisia. 'Let us wish them Godspeed in their struggle,' he said, 'and let us bend all our efforts to the war and the ever more vigorous prosecution of our supreme task.'

23 March 1943, William Summers, *Buffalo Evening News* (New York, US)

Leave China out?

In his broadcast, Churchill had also expressed the hope that the United Nations would form an international organisation to safeguard against further wars, 'headed by the three great victorious Powers, the British Commonwealth of Nations, the United States, and Soviet Russia'. He said that settlements in Europe should be a priority since 'the war against Japan will still be raging', and he spoke of the importance of the 'unity of the three leading victorious Powers'.

Republican Senator Harold Burton questioned Churchill's failure to place China on the same level as Britain, the United States and Russia.

24 March 1943, Howard Fisher, *Oregon Journal* (Portland, US)

Home-breakers, beware!

'I did not become Prime Minister to preside over the liquidation of the Empire . . . The administration of the British colonies must continue to be the sole responsibility of Great Britain.' – Churchill

'They're all mine, and they'll stay mine!'

After the Allied invasion of French North Africa, Churchill said in November 1942 that Britain had 'no acquisitive designs or ambitions in North Africa or any other part of the world. We have not entered this war for profit or expansion, but only for honour'. But, he continued, 'we mean to hold our own. I have not become the King's First Minister in order to preside over the liquidation of the British Empire. For that task, if ever it were prescribed, someone else would have to be found.' Churchill was a staunch imperialist throughout his life, believing that empire was essential to Britain's global power.

The original of this cartoon was given to Churchill and it still hangs in Chartwell today.

24 March 1943, Norman Lindsay, *Bulletin* **(Sydney, Australia)**

Coming together

Axis forces had begun to regroup in Tunisia following
Operation Torch, but on 20 March, the British Eighth Army
launched an attack on the Mareth Line combined with an
advance by New Zealand forces against the Germans' rear.
Axis forces eventually retreated on 28 March. Around the
same time, German forces were falling back in Russia. The
failure at Stalingrad had persuaded the Germans that their
armies in the Caucasus were vulnerable and so they began to
withdraw across the Don. Soviet forces were able to advance
across the Don and reach Kharkiv by mid-February. In
March, the Germans also retreated from their positions facing
Moscow and fell back to Smolensk.

24 March 1943, George Whitelaw, *Daily Herald*

A bar to Easter travel

There were rumours that Rommel, sensing capitulation
was imminent, was starting to evacuate key personnel from
Tunisia. Further reports indicated that Mussolini was pulling
civilians out of Sicily and Sardinia to allow Axis forces to
defend those islands unhampered if an Allied victory in North
Africa led to a landing in Italy. Sicily and Sardinia were already
suffering from heavy Allied air bombardment. It was also
rumoured that Mussolini was making secret preparations to
transfer his government to Florence or Bologna in view of the
threat of an Allied invasion.

11 April 1943, J. C. Walker, *News of the World*

He asks you

On Hitler's fifty-fourth birthday, Goebbels gave a radio broadcast in which he said: 'If one could draw the face of the nation, it would most likely show the changes which we find in the face of the Fuhrer. The furrows of hardness, determination and all the suffering for the people, of endurance and sacrifice, of bitterness and strain have become manifest to every eye. It may sound almost cynical to compare with that the impudent grin which the present chief of the British policy assumes when he appears in public. But it shows who of the two is the more satisfied with war and consequently who wanted it and provoked it. The face alone reveals the guilty man.'

21 April 1943, W. H. Woodburn (Hengest), *Manchester Evening News*

No Prince Charming

In November 1942, the Government published a report of proposed reforms to social services compiled by William Beveridge. Churchill, who knew and had previously collaborated with Beveridge, promised to introduce many of the recommendations in his broadcast on 21 March. But, he warned, the public should not ask him to impose 'great new expenditure on the State without any relation to the circumstances which might prevail at the time' and proposed a 'Four Years' Plan' of post-war reconstruction. The plan would include the introduction of national insurance, a national health service, new housing and education reforms.

5 May 1943, Victor Weisz (Vicky), *News Chronicle*

'What worries them is where we'll meet next.'

On 5 May, Churchill sailed to the US for further talks with Roosevelt and the latter's adviser, Harry Hopkins. It was the latest in a string of foreign trips made by Churchill to, among others, the US, Russia, Egypt, Iran and Turkey, to discuss military strategy and visit British troops, galvanising all with his rhetoric and force of will. Churchill and Roosevelt agreed during the talks that the invasion of Sicily would be their next priority.

When Churchill requested the original of this cartoon from Low as a present for Hopkins, he described it as a cartoon of himself with President Roosevelt sitting on a sofa, 'with a scruffy looking Harry in the background'.

13 May 1943, David Low, *Evening Standard*

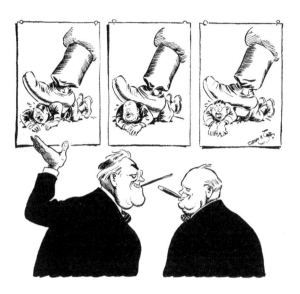

'Did I ever show you my stamps, Winnie?'

Roosevelt inspired nationwide interest in stamp collecting when the White House released numerous photographs of him working on his collection in the 1930s. Throughout his entire life, including his presidency, he spent time each day with his stamps. By the end of his life, his collection amounted to more than one million stamps. Churchill had little interest in Roosevelt's stamp collection.

19 May 1943, Dorman Smith, *Grand Island Independent* (Nebraska, US)

'Have a cigar!'

Tremendous cheering greeted Churchill as he addressed the US Congress on 19 May. He sought to reassure America that Britain would continue the war against Japan, even if Germany surrendered. 'Heavier work lies ahead, not only in the European, but as I have indicated, in the Pacific and Indian spheres,' Churchill predicted. He continued, in a rather bloodthirsty manner: 'It is the duty of those who are charged with the direction of the war to . . . begin the process, so necessary and desirable, of laying the cities and other munitions centres of Japan in ashes, for in ashes they must surely lie before peace comes back to the world.'

21 May 1943, Mick Armstrong, *Herald* (Melbourne, Australia)

Toe-hold

The Axis forces in North Africa surrendered on 13 May, six days after the fall of Tunis. More than 250,000 German and Italian troops were taken prisoner. The battle for North Africa had ended. After this victory, Allied aircraft concentrated their firepower on airfields and industrial targets in Sicily, Sardinia and southern Italy. From early May, the Royal Navy and RAF bombarded the island of Pantelleria, south-west of Sicily and more than 6,000 tons of bombs were dropped. The island garrison surrendered on 11 June and it became a base from which the Allies could launch an invasion of Sicily.

8 June 1943, Sam Wells, *Herald* (Melbourne, Australia)

Invasion where?

The *Daily Herald* reported on 8 June that the Allied policy of keeping the enemy guessing was leading to greater secrecy. It reported that the British Eighth Army had undergone modification and retraining. 'But where it is at present, or where it is likely to be in the future, is not known.' It also reported that 'Italy, who has at least five battleships, will have to gamble her naval power as soon as the Anglo-American landing becomes imminent'. The report quoted the Spanish newspaper *Arriba*: 'Only two objectives could attract this army – the Italian or the Balkan peninsula.'

8 June 1943, George Whitelaw, *Daily Herald*

The usual disagreement between watermelon experts

At their conference in Washington, Churchill and Roosevelt had agreed to postpone a cross-Channel invasion due to a lack of landing craft, most of which were already in use in the Mediterranean. They agreed instead to redirect their forces towards a cross-Channel landing in May 1944, once Italy had been defeated. Stalin had long been pushing for the Allies to open a second front in France to ease pressure on Soviet forces, but Churchill believed that the same objective could be achieved by invading Italy.

29 June 1943, Tom Carlisle, *Dayton Daily News* (Ohio, US)

Well alight!

In spring 1943, Bletchley Park cryptographers finally cracked for good the Enigma code used by German U-boats. This, combined with better long-range aircraft and larger numbers of escorts, turned the tide in the Battle of the Atlantic. In a speech delivered at the Guildhall, London, on 30 June, Churchill told how the Allies had 'hurled their strength at the U-boats.' The result was 'the total defeat of the U-boat attack. More than thirty U-boats were certainly destroyed in the month of May, floundering in many cases with their crews in the dark depths of the sea. Staggered by these deadly losses the U-boats have recoiled to lick their wounds and mourn their dead . . . Since the middle of May scarcely a single merchant ship has been sunk in the whole of the North Atlantic.'

6 July 1943, George Whitelaw, *Daily Herald*

Too late! Too late!

In the early hours of 10 July, the Allies launched Operation Husky, a massive amphibious and airborne assault on the southern shores of Sicily. In the first three days of the invasion, 150,000 troops, 7,000 vehicles, and 300 tanks were landed. The US Seventh Army occupied Palermo by 22 July, cutting Italian forces in the east off from German forces in the west. In August, Allied troops launched the final offensive towards Messina, forcing Axis armies into a narrow strip in the northeast corner of the island from which they evacuated to the Italian mainland. The Allied invasion was completed in just thirty-eight days.

11 July 1943, Stephen Roth, *Sunday Pictorial*

The defeats in North Africa and Sicily, in addition to severe shortages of food, made many Italians desperate to make peace. By this time several members of Mussolini's government had turned against him and, at a meeting of the Grand Council of Fascism on 24–25 July, they called on King Victor Emmanuel III to resume full constitutional authority. The King dismissed Mussolini and appointed Pietro Badoglio as Prime Minister. Churchill told the Commons on 27 July: 'The keystone of the Fascist arch has crumbled, and, without attempting to prophesy, it does not seem unlikely that the entire Fascist edifice will fall to the ground in ruins.'

'Fasces' (from which the term 'fascism' is derived) is a bundle of wooden rods sometimes containing an axe. It was a symbol of law and governance in ancient Rome, before becoming a symbol of the National Fascist Party of Italy.

29 July 1943, W. H. Woodburn (Hengest),
Manchester Evening News

Hamburg-ers

As Churchill had promised Stalin the previous year, the bombing raids in Germany continued with growing intensity. On 24 July, the city of Hamburg was targeted in an operation that lasted eight days. More than 700 RAF and US Air Force aircraft where involved, targeting shipyards, U-boat pens and oil refineries, but also the city centre. The resulting firestorm was one of the largest created by an Allied attack, killing an estimated 37,000 people and destroying 60 per cent of homes. Churchill later described it as 'greater destruction than had ever been suffered by so large a city in so short a time'.

The five-pointed star (seen here on the spatula) was a symbol of the American military.

5 August 1943, Sam Wells, *Herald* **(Melbourne, Australia)**

In early August Churchill crossed the Atlantic once again to meet Roosevelt and the Canadian Prime Minister, William Lyon Mackenzie King, in Quebec City (Roosevelt and Churchill are dressed in the uniform of the Royal Canadian Mounted Police, or 'Mounties'). At the conference, the leaders reiterated their intention to prioritise a cross-Channel landing in May 1944 and from there 'strike at the heart of Germany and destroy her military forces'. They also agreed the details of the invasion of Italy, which would not go much further north than Rome to conserve supplies for the invasion of France.

13 August 1943, Leslie Illingworth, *Daily Mail*

What a carpet to bite!

Hitler's famous rages earned him the nickname *Teppichfresser* – which translates to 'carpet eater'. Historians are undecided about whether Hitler really did chew on carpets in fits of anger, but it is commonly believed that the nickname was taken too literally.

15 August 1943, Stuart Peterson, *Sun* (Sydney, Australia)

'We'll tear your empire to shreds.' – Mr. Churchill, 1942

In December 1940, Churchill had warned the Italian people that the English-speaking world was aroused and was on the march. 'Our armies,' he said, 'are tearing – and will tear – your African Empire to shreds and tatters.' The prophecy came true. At the end of the North African campaign Italy essentially forfeited its African colonies (although the Italian Empire was not formally dissolved until the Treaty of Peace in 1947). With the surrender of Sicily and the fall of Mussolini, the Allies were now planning an invasion of Italy to commence on 3 September.

20 August 1943, Cuthbertson, *Western Mail*

Nothing but bad news

At Quebec, the British Minister of Information, Brendan Bracken, was reported to have said at a press conference: 'Our plans are to bomb, burn and ruthlessly destroy in every way available to us the people responsible for creating this war … When we have rounded up Mr. Hitler, the whole might of the British Empire will be given over to the task of destroying the Japanese. The time will come when Hitler, Tojo, and their gangsters will get to know what is being done at Quebec, and it will be given by admirals, generals, and air marshals.'

21 August 1943, Elmer Messner, *Rochester Times-Union* (New York, US)

'But the thing's illogical!'

The Conservatives almost lost the Chippenham by-election on 24 August to an independent Liberal candidate. At the beginning of the war, the three major parties had agreed that, in a by-election, the party defending the seat would not be challenged by an official candidate from the other parties. There was a growing discontent with this pact and so Dr Donald Johnson, chairman of the Liberal Action Group, decided to stand in Chippenham, arguing that 'democracy should be practised as well as fought for'. He lost by only 195 votes. This cartoon illustrates the extent to which the Conservative Party had come to be defined by Churchill.

27 August 1943, W. H. Woodburn (Hengest), *Manchester Evening News*

The old song

'And so we go singing from one restaurant to the next . . .'

Churchill is again portrayed as a sidekick of Roosevelt's, a mere flag carrier for the American President. The cartoon mocks the Quebec conference as being no more than a talking shop, as the leaders march on to the next conference. The leg braces on Roosevelt's feet are there as a reminder of his physical disability. In 1921, aged thirty-nine, Roosevelt was diagnosed with polio, which left him paralysed from the waist down. He used a wheelchair and leg braces for support for the rest of his life, but he took care to hide his disability from the public.

12 September 1943, Arthur Johnson,
Kladderadatsch **(Berlin, Germany)**

Winnie's not worried about a post-war job

During his North America trip, Churchill travelled to Harvard University to receive an honorary degree. He used his speech there on 6 September to stress the need for continued Anglo-American unity. 'There never has been anything like it between two allies,' he declared. 'Now in my opinion it would be a most foolish and improvident act to break up this smooth-running and immensely powerful machinery the moment the war is over. For our own safety, as well as for the security of the rest of the world, we are bound to keep it working and in running order after the war – probably for a good many years . . . If we are together nothing is impossible. If we are divided all will fail.'

16 September 1943, Dorman Smith, *Grand Island Independent* **(Nebraska, US)**

Imitation the sincerest flattery

On 3 September, the Italian government signed an armistice agreement with the Allies. When the Nazis learned of the pact, they responded by attacking Italian forces and taking most of the north and centre of Italy. Hitler gave a speech on 10 September claiming that the Italian defection meant little to Germany. In a defiant tone reminiscent of Churchill in 1940 (when it was thought that an invasion of Britain was imminent), Hitler declared that the Allies will 'never break the steel ring forged by the German homeland and held in heroism and blood by our soldiers . . . Let every single German, wherever he may be, realise that the existence of our people and the fate of future generations depend on himself and his efforts and his willingness to sacrifice.'

5 October 1943, David Low, *Evening Standard*

'United Notions'

Senior diplomats from the US, Britain and the Soviet Union gathered for talks at the Kremlin from 18 October to 11 November. They discussed co-operation in the war effort and agreed to create a new world organisation. The participants then issued the Moscow Declarations, which set out how their goals were to be achieved. In its 'Statement on Atrocities', all nations declared that after any armistice with Germany, those individuals suspected of war crimes in various countries would be returned to those countries for trial and punishment.

Later in November, the leaders of the 'Big Three' countries – Roosevelt, Churchill and Stalin – met for the first time, at a conference held at the Soviet embassy in Tehran. The three leaders also spoke about the post-war world order, including the need for a United Nations organisation and the division of Germany into smaller states.

3 November 1943, Mick Armstrong, *Herald* (Melbourne, Australia)

At the Lord Mayor's banquet

The soup course

In early November, Hitler and Churchill gave speeches only a day apart – Hitler at the Löwenbräukeller in Munich and Churchill at the Mansion House, London. Churchill claimed that 1943 had so far been a 'year of almost unbroken victory' and spoke of the importance of 'food, work and homes' for all in the post-war peace. Hitler, on the other hand, pleaded with his audience to give their utmost to the war effort, saying: 'Whatever the sacrifices we must make now, they are incomparable with what we should have to bear if we lose the war.' He also acknowledged the Allied propaganda, which emphasised imminent victory and post-war planning, and said 'he did not know' if there were Germans who hoped for an Allied victory. The *Bradford Observer* commented: 'No two speeches on the same theme could furnish a more instructive contrast.'

10 November 1943, George Middleton, *Bradford Observer*

Haggling over Europe

'That could suit them!'

Goebbels changed the focus of the German propaganda campaign to depict Germany as the defenders of 'Western European culture' against the 'Bolshevist hordes'. This cartoon portrays Churchill and Roosevelt betraying Europe by sending it blindly to the Bolshevik butcher, here represented by Stalin.

14 November 1943, Oskar Garvens,
Kladderadatsch (Berlin, Germany)

The boys are doing O. K.!

Churchill and Roosevelt returned from the Tehran conference via Cairo, where they met Turkey's President İnönü. Churchill tried to persuade İnönü that Turkey should enter the war on the side of the Allies, believing that Bulgaria, Romania and Hungary would then fall out of the Axis sphere of influence. But İnönü was reluctant to commit without assurances that the Allies would provide financial and military aid and that the US and Britain would support Turkey in case of a Soviet invasion of the Turkish Straits. With preparations for an Allied landing in northern France now in full swing, Churchill and Roosevelt were reluctant to commit to either. Turkey would not enter the war until February 1945.

8 December 1943, Cy Hungerford, *Pittsburgh Post-Gazette* (Philadelphia, US)

Goebbels raged over the RAF's use of phosphorus bombs – incendiary devices that burst into flames on impact – in raids on Berlin. He said in a speech at a Berlin cinema on 28 November: 'As England fought in the First World War with the hunger blockade, so today she fights with phosphorus and fire against women and children who in their defence-lessness are naturally more remunerative targets than armed German soldiers. After other great cities, it is now the German capital's turn. The enemy smothers it with high-explosive and incendiary bombs, unloads masses of phosphorus canisters on its cultural monuments, hospitals, churches and workers' districts.'

24 December 1943, artist unknown, *Volk en Vaderland* (Utrecht, Netherlands)

On the way home from his exhausting month-long trip to the conferences in Cairo and Tehran, Churchill contracted pneumonia. He also suffered two mild heart attacks while being treated in Carthage and Churchill's doctor feared he might die. Churchill responded 'If I die, don't worry. The war is won.' Nevertheless, he continued to receive visitors and hosted a Christmas Day conference of five Commanders-in-Chief in his dressing gown.

On 26 December, the German battleship *Scharnhorst* was sunk by British cruisers protecting a merchant convoy on the northern route to Russia. Only thirty-six of its almost 2,000-strong crew survived.

28 December 1943, Leslie Illingworth, *Daily Mail*

1944

Celebrating – and how!

In early January, the American politician Wendell Wilkie wrote a piece in the *New York Times* arguing that one of the most important issues of the time was Russia's intentions towards its neighbours. *Pravda*, the Communist Party newspaper, replied that the matter was an 'internal affair of the Soviet Union, in which [Wilkie] should not interfere'. The *New York Times* commented that *Pravda*'s response was 'a warning to Britain and America to keep their hands off Poland and other states whose borders the Red Army was nearing'.

The Atlantic Charter – a statement of post-war goals issued by Britain and the US in August 1941 – had declared that no nation should seek territorial aggrandisement.

7 January 1944, Cy Hungerford, *Pittsburgh Post-Gazette* (Philadelphia, US)

The finishing touches

Hitler and Churchill were both keen painters. Hitler had tried to make a living as a painter during his Vienna years but had very little commercial or critical success (and foreign propagandists regularly belittled him as a house decorator). Churchill had taken to painting after the Gallipoli campaign of 1915–16 and his subsequent fall from grace. He only created one painting during the war, a view of Marrakesh and the Atlas Mountains, but this was painted during the Casablanca conference in January 1943 – not, as this cartoon claims, during his later convalescence.

In September 1943, Albert Speer, the German Minister of Armaments, had publicly promised that he would use a 'secret weapon' as retribution for the mass bombing of German cities. It was known to the Allies that Germany was working to develop the world's first long-range guided missile.

19 January 1944, J. C. Walker, *Western Mail*

*'Oi, that's **my** property!'*

At a by-election in Brighton, the Conservative candidate, Flight-Lieutenant William Teeling, was expected to be unopposed for the seat. Bruce Dutton Briant, brother of Brighton's mayor, entered the election at the last moment as an independent candidate. His claim that he gave 'wholehearted support to Churchill and the Government in the task of winning the war' provoked Churchill to write that he was sure the electors would not be 'taken in by this attempted swindle' and that this was 'no time for political antics'. Teeling won the election with a significantly reduced Conservative majority, which was blamed on Churchill's intervention.

3 February 1944, W. H. Woodburn (Hengest), *Manchester Evening News*

*'I reckon a drop or two of this will send
him flying one way or the other.'*

Spain technically remained neutral throughout the war, but
it was well known that the country's leader, Francisco Franco,
had met Hitler several times to offer support. Franco also
assisted Germany and Italy – which had backed him in the
Spanish Civil War – by secretly exporting minerals such as
tungsten, iron ore and zinc, that were essential for armament
production.

After a long period of unheeded protests, Churchill and
Roosevelt decided to take the drastic step of introducing an
oil embargo to persuade Franco's government to cease its
tungsten exports and remain genuinely neutral.

13 February 1944, Stephen Roth, *Sunday Pictorial*

The intruder

Charles Frederick White won a by-election in West Derbyshire,
defeating the Conservative candidate, the Marquess of
Hartington, by more than 4,500 votes. White had stood down
from the Labour Party before running, thereby evading the
wartime ban on standing against the incumbent party. The
defeat was particularly surprising as the Marquess's family (who
owned the nearby Chatsworth estate) had represented the constituency almost continuously since 1885. According to Hannen
Swaffer in *John Bull*: 'The West Derby result proves that if there
were now a General Election in which a Popular Front were
formed of all the parties on the left, the Tories would suffer a
crushing defeat – even with Mr. Churchill as their leader.'

19 February 1944, Talbot Ellison, *Birmingham Mail*

The obstruction

Following the signing of the Molotov–Ribbentrop Pact in 1939, the Soviet Union invaded eastern Poland at the same time as Germany invaded the west. The result was the splitting of Poland along the Curzon Line (so named because it was first proposed by Lord Curzon, the Foreign Secretary, at the end of the First World War). Now that the Soviets had joined the Allies, Churchill and Roosevelt privately agreed with Stalin that Poland's western border should remain at the Curzon Line. Poland would be compensated with land from Germany. The Polish government, exiled in London, refused to agree to this arrangement. The Polish newspaper *Dziennik Polski* declared: 'If Poland is deprived of almost half her territory and nearly 11 millions of her people to the advantage of another of the United Nations, it cannot be regarded by the Polish people as a just act or a rational solution of Polish-Russian relations on a really peaceful and permanently friendly basis.'

2 March 1944, Jimmy Friell (Gabriel), *Daily Worker*

The small disagreement

'What are you saying? That you are the one who supports me? No, I'm the one supporting you!'

This German cartoon once again emphasises Roosevelt's disability and the unequal power balance between Britain and the United States. The latter was beginning to increasingly dominate the Allied war strategy, especially for the imminent D-Day landings, which had been Roosevelt's preferred course of action (this was, of course, unknown to the cartoonist). Despite the depiction here, German cartoons focusing on Roosevelt's physical disability were surprisingly rare.

5 April 1944, Olaf Gulbransson,
Simplicissimus **(Munich, Germany)**

Guessing

Churchill broadcast to the nation on 26 March, in the run-up to the D-Day landings. He said: 'The hour of our greatest effort and action is approaching ... The magnificent armies of the United States are here, or are pouring in. Our own troops, the best trained and best equipped we have ever had, stand at their side.' He also warned that 'in order to deceive and baffle the enemy as well as to exercise the forces, there will be many false alarms, many feints and many dress rehearsals'. In late 1943, the Allies had approved Operation Bodyguard, a campaign to spread misinformation about the timing and location of an Allied attack. The campaign included recruiting double agents and creating a fictitious army under General Patton stationed in Kent.

20 April 1944, Will Mahony, *Daily Telegraph* (Sydney, Australia)

'Let's see if it's soft enough now, Ike.'

The Allied strategy was to force Germany to commit the maximum number of infantry divisions in Italy (which Churchill had previously called the 'soft underbelly' of Europe) at the same time as the cross-Channel invasion. Plans were, therefore, put in place for an advance towards Rome. Churchill believed that if thirty-four German divisions could be kept in the Mediterranean then it would make an 'immense contribution' to the Normandy operation, which was being prepared by the supreme commander of Allied forces in Western Europe, General Dwight D. Eisenhower (nicknamed 'Ike').

The black eagle features on the coat of arms of Germany. It was adapted as the symbol of the Nazi Party by adding a laurel wreath with a swastika at its centre.

26 April 1944, Jacob Burck, *Chicago Daily Times* (Illinois, US)

Unconditional surrender

The Atlantic Charter, drawn up by the US and Britain in 1941, was a plan for a new world order that respected 'the right of all peoples to choose the form of government under which they will live'. Churchill, a staunch imperialist, insisted that these principles should not apply to British colonies. Roosevelt disagreed but was reluctant to force the issue. Mahatma Gandhi wrote to Roosevelt to explain that 'the Allied declaration that the Allies are fighting to make the world safe for the freedom of the individual and for democracy sounds hollow so long as India and, for that matter, Africa are exploited by Great Britain'.

26 April 1944, Carl Somdal, *Chicago Tribune* (US)

Speak up, gentlemen

From 1–16 May, Churchill hosted the first Commonwealth Prime Ministers' Conference. It was attended by the leaders of all the nations within the Commonwealth, with the exceptions of Ireland and Newfoundland (which did not become part of Canada until 1949). During the conference, the prime ministers of five nations (Britain, Australia, New Zealand, Canada and South Africa) issued a declaration in which they said that they hoped 'when the storm and passions of war have passed away, all countries now overrun by the enemy shall be free to decide for themselves their future form of democratic government'.

On 17 April, the Allied Supreme Headquarters had given the green light for a pre-invasion air offensive against German airfields and railways in Normandy. The goal was to isolate the designated invasion area.

2 May 1944, Will Mahony, *Daily Telegraph* **(Sydney, Australia)**

First of all, gentlemen, welcome to our right little, tight little island.

By the time of the Commonwealth conference, southern England resembled a vast military camp in preparation for D-Day. The Normandy landings were to be the largest amphibious invasion in history. The invasion fleet comprised nearly 7,000 vessels and 11,000 aircraft were made available. In the first wave, 156,000 Allied troops from twelve nations would cross the Channel by boat, with another 23,000 airborne troops being dropped into France. But that was just the beginning. By the end of June, more than 850,000 men, 148,000 vehicles and 570,000 tons of supplies had landed in northern France.

'Tight Little Island' is a patriotic folk song originating from the eighteenth century. The cartoon quotes from the lines *'Oh! what a snug little Island,/ A right little, tight little Island!/ All the globe round, none can be found/ So happy as this little Island.'*

2 May 1944, David Ghilchik, *Daily Sketch*

The Allied misinformation campaign continued to mask the real landing plans. Operation Fortitude was devised to make it seem as though the Allies intended a dual invasion of Norway and Calais. A fictional British Fourth Army and a phantom First US Army Group were conceived, based in Edinburgh and Kent respectively. Fake radio signals were used to give the impression of large Allied forces stationed there. The plan was so successful that the Germans maintained forces in Calais for some weeks after the Normandy landing, just in case.

'Can I do you now, sir' was the catchphrase of Mrs Mopp, a charlady played by Dorothy Summers in the hugely popular BBC radio wartime comedy series *It's That Man Again*.

9 May 1944, Cyril Price (Kim), *Daily Sketch*

(left) The Churchill touch (right) '. . . drawing rude caricatures of General Franco'

Churchill, to the surprise and dismay of many, stood up in the House of Commons on
24 May and praised the Fascist leadership of General Franco. He commended Spain for
keeping out of the war and thanked them for not bending to the German request to seize
Gibraltar, nor interfering in Allied operations in North Africa. He also looked forward
'to increasingly good relations with Spain'. Churchill then appealed to all cartoonists to stop
drawing 'comical or even rude caricatures' of Franco and rebuked those who 'think it clever,
and even funny, to insult and abuse the Government of Spain'.

(left) 26 May 1944, George Whitelaw, *Daily Herald*
(right) 25 May 1944, Victor Weisz (Vicky), *News Chronicle*

A man of his word

In the early hours of 6 June, the first airborne troops dropped into Normandy. They were followed by the first beach landings at 6.30am. The massive Allied invasion was so unexpected that Rommel was visiting family and most senior German officers were away on anti-invasion training. It was some hours before the Germans gathered their forces to repel the invaders. At 10 o'clock that morning BBC radio announcer John Snagge announced: 'D-Day has come. Early this morning the Allies began the assault on the north-western face of Hitler's European Fortress.' By the following morning the German forces on the beaches had been defeated at the cost of more than 4,000 Allied lives. The public excitement at the operation was so great that, on 8 June, Churchill advised MPs in the Commons to 'give strong warnings against over-optimism'.

8 June 1944, Ed Huxtable, *Toronto Daily Star* **(Ontario, Canada)**

'OY!' (Mr. Churchill, asked in Parliament yesterday whether
he intends to visit the Norman Front, gave no reply.)

While updating the Commons on 8 June on the Normandy landings, Churchill declined to reveal whether he intended to visit Allied troops in France. In fact, he had wanted to be present on the bridge of HMS *Belfast* on D-Day, much to the annoyance of Eisenhower. He was only dissuaded when King George VI said to him: 'Well, as long as you feel that it is desirable to go along, I think it is my duty to go along with you!' It was not until six days after D-Day that Churchill visited Normandy, and four days later the King followed him. Churchill travelled on board HMS *Kelvin* and made sure that the ship fired on German positions while he was on the bridge.

9 June 1944, George Whitelaw, *Daily Herald*

Return of Winston the Conqueror

A coastal strip sixty miles long had been seized by Allied forces and the clash of men and arms in Normandy was reverberating throughout the world. Winston Churchill spent some time with the troops and his commanders.

The *Yorkshire Post* reported on 13 June on Churchill's visit to Normandy. 'It was the most dramatic arrival of Mr Churchill in any front-line war theatre. A grey-green "duck" slowly climbed up the yellow sands and out stepped Churchill. Soldiers busily engaged in unloading landing craft stood in blank amazement. They couldn't believe their eyes. Then they recognised the familiar Trinity House cap, the cigar and the two fingers raised in a "V" sign. "Blimey, it's Churchill himself," one private shouted to his mate.'

The cartoon mimics the Bayeux Tapestry, which depicts the events of the Norman conquest of England in 1066.

14 June 1944, Gordon Minhinnick,
New Zealand Herald (**Auckland**)

Recognition difficulties

Churchill and Roosevelt had come to regard Charles de Gaulle with some suspicion (in particular Roosevelt, who considered De Gaulle an 'apprentice dictator') and refused to acknowledge a provisional government in France until elections had been held. When Churchill suggested that De Gaulle should improve his relationship with Roosevelt, De Gaulle responded that he did not intend to 'lodge my candidacy for power in France with Roosevelt; the French government exists'. De Gaulle travelled to Normandy on 14 June, eight days after the landings. He nominated Bayeux as the new capital of Free France and gave a speech in the town that was so enthusiastically received that it helped to demonstrate the legitimacy of De Gaulle's leadership.

15 June 1944, George Middleton, *Birmingham Gazette*

Very unfair, Herr Churchill! (On the left:) 'Even military idiots find it
difficult not to see some faults in some of Cpl. Hitler's actions.' (On the
right:) 'Gosh, what a lie, it's not him, it's the generals!'

In his report to the House of Commons on 2 August, Churchill praised the Russian forces for having 'done the main work in tearing the guts out of the German army'. He did concede that 'it may well be that the Russian success has been somewhat aided by the strategy of Herr Hitler – of Corporal Hitler. Even military idiots find it difficult not to see some faults in some of his actions.' In June, at the same time as the Normandy landings, the Soviet army launched a massive attack on the German forces in Belorussian territory. Around 2.3 million Soviets attacked fewer than 800,000 Germans, shattering the enemy line. It was the biggest defeat in German military history, with more than 450,000 German casualties. By July the Russian army had taken Minsk and western Ukraine.

4 August 1944, Joseph Flatter, *Spectator*

*An English newspaper asks when the time will come
when Churchill will have to include Bolshevists
in his cabinet . . . 'Soon it will be time!'*

As a German defeat seemed ever more likely, their cartoonists focused on the ramifications of the spread of Bolshevism,
presenting an apocalyptic vision of what would happen if
the Soviets won the war. Stalin's intentions in Poland were
becoming an increasing cause for concern among the Allies as
well. The Soviet leader had announced the formation of the
Polish Committee of National Liberation, excluding the exiled
Polish Government. Sensing a new threat, on 31 July the Poles
rose in revolt against the German army, hoping to free Warsaw
before the Soviets arrived. Churchill appealed to Stalin to help
the Poles with ammunition and supplies. Stalin refused.

20 August 1944, Arthur Johnson,
Kladderadatsch (**Berlin, Germany**)

Revival

The Allies continued to advance across northern France through June and July. The Germans withdrew from city after city and, on 25 August, Paris was liberated. On 15 August, the Allies had also orchestrated a second invasion at Provence, where the weakened German forces began to fall back after just two days. The whole German army began to retreat to the Siegfried Line, a line of defences constructed opposite the French Maginot Line in the 1930s and which stretched almost 400 miles from the border with the Netherlands to the Swiss frontier in the south.

'We're Going to Hang out the Washing on the Siegfried Line' was a popular morale-boosting song written by Captain Jimmy Kennedy in 1939.

29 August 1944, William Pidgeon (Wep),
Daily Telegraph (Sydney, Australia)

'Hi, there! Put that light on!'

With the public growing more confident of victory, there were calls for the Government to focus on post-war reforms, such as introducing national insurance and a national health service. Labour MP Edgar Granville was reported in the press as saying: 'What we need is a small Cabinet of fresh, first-class brains for post-war preparations free from the major responsibilities of running the final stages of the war and clearing up Europe.' Meanwhile, since the Normandy landings, Britain had been facing an almost constant attack from German V-1 flying bombs, leading to night-time blackouts. On 8 September London was hit by the first V-2 bomb – the world's first long-range ballistic missile.

10 September 1944, Stephen Roth, *Sunday Pictorial*

Victory special

Churchill sailed to Canada for another conference with Roosevelt and the Combined Chiefs of Staff in Quebec, starting on 12 September. Wearing a naval uniform and smoking a cigar, he smiled broadly through be-flagged streets on his way to the venue. He gave the crowds the V-sign and told them 'Victory is everywhere'. The main subject of the conference was the post-war plan for a defeated Germany, the continuation of the Lend-Lease agreement and the development of the atom bomb.

12 September 1944, Will Mahony,
***Daily Telegraph* (Sydney, Australia)**

Let him wear it!

During the conference, Churchill and Roosevelt initially welcomed a plan by Henry Morgenthau, the US Treasury Secretary, which proposed both the demilitarisation and deindustrialisation of Germany. The plan involved destroying all industries in the Ruhr, Germany's industrial heartland, and converting Germany to a 'primarily agricultural and pastoral' economy. The plan was ultimately abandoned after it was leaked to the press and met with fierce criticism. But it was immediately seized upon by German propaganda as an example of potential Allied retribution. Goebbels said that the plan would turn Germany into a giant 'potato field'.

5 October 1944, W. H. Woodburn (Hengest), *Manchester Evening News*

Getting a few things off their chests

Churchill visited Moscow for talks with Stalin on 9 October. Churchill wanted to discuss the future of Poland, where the insurgence had recently been crushed. He had told the Commons on 28 September that he thought there was a solution in which 'Russia gets the security which she is entitled to have' and 'the Polish nation have restored to them national sovereignty and independence'. He also wanted to discuss the future of Greece and Yugoslavia, hoping to prevent them also falling under Communist control. While at the conference in Moscow, Churchill drew up what he later called his 'naughty document' (but became known as the 'Percentages Agreement'). This was a proposal to divide Europe into Western and Russian spheres of influence.

17 October 1944, Dorman Smith, *Grand Island Independent* (Nebraska, US)

Keeping it going

(To-day the Premier will move the prolongation of the life of Parliament.)

Churchill spoke in the Commons on 31 October during the debate on the Prolongation of Parliament Act 1944 – the fourth act to extend the life of the current
Parliament during the war. Churchill said that he was 'clearly of the opinion that
the coalition of parties ought not to be broken before Nazidom is broken', but
that it would be 'wrong to continue this Parliament beyond the period of the
German war'. He spoke passionately about the rights of the people and that 'at the
bottom of all the tributes paid to democracy, is the little man, walking into the
little booth, with a little pencil, making a little cross on a little bit of paper – no
amount of rhetoric or voluminous discussion can possibly palliate the overwhelming importance of that point.'

31 October 1944, George Whitelaw, *Daily Herald*

Protracted embrace

Churchill accepted an invitation from De Gaulle – who had
formed an interim French administration – to visit Paris.
Churchill and De Gaulle were greeted by thousands of
cheering Parisians. In his speech, De Gaulle admitted that
Paris would not have been liberated 'if our old and gallant
ally England . . . had not deployed the extraordinary determination to win, and that magnificent courage which saved the
freedom of the world'. A few days previously, the *Manchester
Evening News* reported that a disagreement had broken out
between De Gaulle and the French Communist Party over the
disarming of militiamen. The Communists claimed that De
Gaulle's interim government was 'anti-democratic and aims at
personal power' and the dissolution of the militias was part of
an 'anti-Communist campaign'.

6 November 1944, W. H. Woodburn (Hengest),
Manchester Evening News

The production manager

Churchill received a government White Paper on Britain's total war production since the start of the war. According to the *Lancashire Daily Post*: 'We mobilised more than 22,000,000 men and women for the forces, civil defence, and war industry, under bomb and shell, in blacked-out factory and shipyard. We, "the average man and woman", turned out 100,000 aircraft, 5,000 tanks, 35,000 guns, built 5,700 Navy ships and millions of tons of merchant shipping. We spent £695,000,000,000, or £158 10s every second of those five years.'

1 December 1944, William Furnival, *Lancashire Daily Post*

Time to get going

Churchill had made an unofficial pact with Stalin at the Moscow conference about the limits of Communist influence in post-war Europe, but it was becoming clear that the spread of Communism was not so easily checked. Churchill reported that Tito (the recently recognised Communist prime minister of Yugoslavia) had 'turned very nasty' and was 'thinking now only of grabbing Trieste, Istria, Fiume etc'. Meanwhile, trouble was brewing in Greece. After the German withdrawal, the Allies had brought together the royalist and Communist resistance in an uneasy coalition government. But on 3 December, a civil war broke out when the Communist guerrilla groups refused to disband. Churchill ordered for military reinforcements to be sent from Italy 'without the slightest delay'.

A meeting between the 'Big Three' was expected but no definite date had yet been fixed.

Churchill wrote to Harry Hopkins, Roosevelt's closest adviser: 'It grieves me very much to see signs of our drifting apart at a time when unity becomes ever more important, as danger recedes and faction arises.'

12 December 1944, Anne Mergen, *Dayton Daily News* (Ohio, US)

War is paved with broken pledges

President Roosevelt was re-elected for an unprecedented fourth term in November and his popularity remained high, partly due to US military successes. But there were segments of the American public that objected to the vast quantities of men and materiel being sent to the European front. Thanks to the Lend-Lease arrangements, in 1944 the United States government spent, collected and borrowed more money than in any other year in its history. According to a statement from the United States Treasury, expenditure exceeded $24 billion, and the national debt reached $58 billion. More than 29,000 American men had been killed during the Normandy landings, and more than 400,000 would die during the war.

30 December 1944, John McCutcheon,
Chicago Tribune (Illinois, US)

We all remember those broken pledges.

And here is another one to be remembered.

1945

Greek monument – restored A.D. 1945

A brutal civil war had erupted in Athens and British troops and Greek police struggled to maintain order in the city. On Christmas Day 1944, Churchill had flown into Athens to preside over a conference with the major parties, but no settlement was reached. By early January, British forces managed to repress the Communist forces in Athens with great difficulty and at the cost of thousands of men, but by then the Communist forces had formed strongholds in the north of Greece. On 15 January, General Scobie, the British commander, agreed to a ceasefire and General Nikolaos Plastiras was installed as prime minister.

19 January 1945, George Butterworth, *Daily Dispatch*

Caviar!

Churchill, Roosevelt and Stalin agreed to meet at Yalta in the Crimea from 4 February to discuss the post-war reorganisation of Europe. In recent days Soviet forces had made massive gains on the Eastern Front. On 17 January they entered Warsaw and from there they advanced rapidly, taking the Baltic states, Danzig and East Prussia. Within two weeks they were only 40 miles from Berlin.

31 January 1945, Anne Mergen, *Dayton Daily News* **(Ohio, US)**

'As a matter of fact there is something on my mind!'

Recognising that the war in the Pacific was likely to continue long after the defeat of Germany, one of the main talking points at Yalta was the conditions under which the Soviet Union would join Britain and the US in declaring war on Japan. It was agreed that, if Russia were to enter the war, it would be granted possession of southern Sakhalin and the Kuril Islands held by Japan, as well as a sphere of influence in Manchuria.

7 February 1945, George Butterworth, *Daily Dispatch*

No, Sir!

Mr. Churchill has bluntly rejected the Spanish Dictator Franco's claims to sit at the peace conference.

While Churchill was at Yalta, Franco suggested not only an Anglo-Spanish alliance in the face of what he saw as the growing Soviet threat, but also offered to act as mediator for a negotiated peace between Germany and Britain. Churchill bluntly turned down both of the Communist dictator's proposals.

13 February 1945, Ian Gall, *Courier-Mail* (Brisbane, Australia)

'Where are they? Gone? Let this pernicious hour stand aye
accursed in the calendar!' – Macbeth IV, I

The leaders of the Big Three nations decided at the Yalta conference that Germany would be divided into four occupied zones, one for each of the three nations, plus one for France. Germany was to be completely demilitarised and war criminals were to be punished. The conference also set up a 'Committee on Dismemberment of Germany' to decide whether it should be split into several nations to limit its power in the post-war world. The German official news agency reported: 'The annihilation mania of Europe's enemies has now assumed the shape of a final programme . . . the statement was signed by the three main war criminals, Churchill, Roosevelt and Stalin, clearly imbued with the spirit of Jewish hatred.'

15 February 1945, Cyril Price (Kim), *Daily Sketch*

The thin anti-red line

Another of the issues that dominated at Yalta was the fate of Poland. Churchill pushed for democratic governments in all the Eastern European states, and pointed out that Britain had gone to war so that Poland could be 'free and sovereign'. Stalin insisted that the Soviets would retain the Polish territory they had claimed in 1939 – and which they were already occupying – but that he intended to hold elections in the region (a promise that would be broken over the coming months). The conference accepted the deal. Churchill returned to much criticism from the Conservative Party that Poland had been betrayed. On 27 February, Churchill assured the Commons that it was 'the fairest division of territory that can in all the circumstances be made', but ended by saying that the Great Powers 'must seek to serve and not to rule'.

27 February 1945, Victor Weisz (Vicky), *News Chronicle*

Doing the Salome Walk

In the Australian parliament, Labor MP Donald Mountjoy described this cartoon as 'a derogatory caricature of Mr Churchill dancing before Marshal Stalin to music played by President Roosevelt', and asked the Minister for Information to prevent the publication of such propaganda. He was told that, under a new censorship code, the government could only prevent publication if the material affected the nation's security. 'The *Bulletin* has published many articles and cartoons that have certainly not assisted the war effort and have probably injured it,' Mountjoy said. 'It is undoubtedly the most anti-Australian of all Australian newspapers.'

28 February 1945, Ted Scofield, *Bulletin* (Sydney, Australia)

You can't trust your own shadow!

On 3 March, Churchill stood on German territory for the first time since 1932. In early 1945, after the final major German offensive at the Battle of the Bulge failed, the last of the Siegfried Line bunkers was captured. Churchill went first to visit the US Ninth Army at Jülich before being driven to survey the captured Siegfried Line. British General Brooke, Chief of the Imperial General Staff, wrote of that moment: 'I shall never forget the childish grin of intense satisfaction that spread all over his face.'

8 March 1945, George Whitelaw, *Daily Herald*

While at the Siegfried Line, Churchill gave encouragement to the US and British troops who continued fighting towards the Rhine. He said: 'Anyone can see that one good, strong heave all together will bring the war in Europe to an end.' He also told a Highland division that its war 'began with a terrible disaster, but its soul rose again, and those who had struck it down have been themselves defeated and see nothing but ruin before them.' When he visited the First Canadian Army on 4 March, Churchill chalked onto a giant shell the words 'Hitler Personally', then fired it at one of the main German escape routes across the Rhine.

8 March 1945, Ian Gall, *Courier-Mail* (Brisbane, Australia)

The old gag (up to date)

Two thousand delegates attended the annual Conservative Party conference at Westminster Central Hall and unanimously carried, amid cheering, a resolution expressing deep gratitude to Churchill for his war leadership. Rab Butler, Minister of Education, said that, unlike the Labour Party, Conservative policies were 'not written for us by cloud-capped theorists and then endorsed by a Party caucus'. He also said: 'We look to the master builder and offer him our help in this, his latest and greatest work – our national reconstruction.' The temptation for the party to fight an election – which would come within four months – on the strength of Churchill's personality and popularity alone was too great.

14 March 1945, George Middleton, *Birmingham Gazette*

Political divisions began to resurface in Britain as the country looked forward to the end of the war. Churchill, perhaps sensing that the tide of public opinion was turning against his party, hinted at the Conservative conference that a second coalition government could be formed, at least until the defeat of Japan, if the Conservatives won the next general election. Clement Attlee, leader of the Labour Party, insisted that the party would take no part in a coalition government once the war was won.

20 March 1945, Victor Weisz (Vicky), *News Chronicle*

Watch on the Rhine

On 24 March, Churchill travelled into Germany to watch Montgomery's offensive across the Rhine. Churchill insisted on driving the full
length of the offensive line from Xanten, through Marienbaum, to high
ground at Kalkar to watch the crossing of the 51st Highland Division.
The next day, Churchill crossed the river with Montgomery and senior
American officers but came within fifty yards of being hit by a German
artillery shell while viewing the Ninth Army's bridgehead. 'The Rhine and
all its fortresses line behind the 21st Group of Armies,' Churchill wrote
in Montgomery's message book. 'A beaten army, not long ago Master of
Europe, retreats before its pursuers. The goal is not long to be denied
those who have come so far and fought so well . . . Forward on all wings
of flame to final Victory.'

27 March 1945, Ian Gall, *Courier-Mail* (Brisbane, Australia)

New pardner

On 7 April, the Minister of Labour, Ernest Bevin, used his first political speech since the start of the war to criticise the Conservative record in government. The Labour MP insisted victory in war would not be down to a 'one-man war or a one-man Government' and that the Conservatives had 'brought the nation to the verge of disaster' by failing to rearm after the last war. He added that the nation 'deserved the chance to decide the policy that should be followed in peace and reconstruction'. Bevin concluded: 'I have a profound admiration for the Prime Minister as a national leader … but I have never given it to him as leader of the Conservative Party.'

9 April 1945, Leslie Illingworth, *Daily Mail*

President Franklin D. Roosevelt died on 12 April aged sixty-three of a sudden cerebral haemorrhage. Churchill wrote to Harry Hopkins that he felt 'a very painful personal loss' and, when delivering a tribute in the House of Commons, said: 'Victory had cast its sure and steady beam upon him.' Harry Truman took over as President – a man who Churchill had never met and who had been Vice President for only eighty-two days. On becoming president, Truman promised 'to begin work on a permanent peace treaty' to prevent future wars, and defined his task as that of winning the war and framing a peace that would work. 'That,' he said, 'is all I shall devote my life to from now on.'

16 April 1945, W. H. Woodburn (Hengest),
Manchester Evening News

Waiting

On 29 April, the German armies in Italy surrendered. Two days later, Hitler's death was announced on German radio; he had committed suicide. Mussolini had been executed three days prior. On 3 May, more than half a million German soldiers surrendered to Montgomery's army, followed by 'far more than a million' (according to Churchill) the next day. With the total surrender of Germany imminent, Churchill was asked if he had any statement to make about the cessation of hostilities in Europe. He replied that he 'had no special statement to make, except that it was definitely more satisfactory than it was this time five years ago'.

4 May 1945, William Furnival, *Lancashire Daily Post*

WIN

The surrender of the German armies was ratified on May 8, 1945.

At 3pm on 8 May, almost five years to the day since he became Prime Minister, Churchill broadcast to the nation that the war with Germany was over. The day was to be known as Victory in Europe day. Churchill appeared on the balcony at Buckingham Palace with the royal family before driving to Whitehall to address the crowd from the Ministry of Health balcony. To ecstatic crowds, he said: 'God bless you all. This is your victory.' To which the crowds shouted back: 'No – it's yours.'

11 May 1945, Gordon Minhinnick,
***New Zealand Herald* (Auckland)**

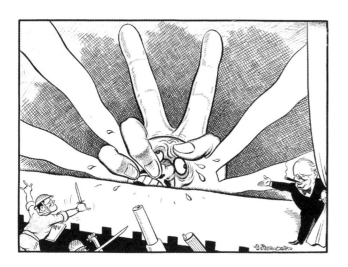

The stage is set

Amid all the revelry, Churchill reminded the nation that they remained at war with Japan. 'We may allow ourselves a brief period of rejoicing,' Churchill said during his VE Day broadcast, 'but let us not forget for a moment the toil and the efforts that lie ahead. Japan, with all her treachery and greed, remains unsubdued. The injury she has inflicted on Great Britain, the United States, and other countries, and her detestable cruelties, call for justice and retribution. We must now devote all our strength and resources to the completion of our task both at home and abroad. Advance, Britannia!'

14 May 1945, George Butterworth, *Daily Dispatch*

The Labour Party conference was held in Blackpool from 21 May. Churchill had already proposed to Clement Attlee that the wartime coalition should continue until Japan was defeated. Attlee privately said that he was 'favourably disposed' to the arrangement. However, when put to the Labour Party conference, the motion was met with hostility. The delegates were eager to return to party politics. Attlee wrote to Churchill to confirm that his party would leave the coalition immediately.

22 May 1945, Leslie Illingworth, *Daily Mail*

Winnie fits them all

Realising that the coalition government was now dead, Churchill went to Buckingham Palace on 23 May to tender his resignation to the King. There was now to be a general election for the first time in ten years. King George asked Churchill to form a caretaker government until an election could be held and votes from servicemen serving abroad could be counted. Churchill formed a temporary Conservative administration but set an election date for 5 July; he was under pressure from his party to announce a quick election to exploit his standing as the man who won the war.

23 May 1945, Jerry Doyle, *Philadelphia Inquirer* (US)

He is used to blood, toil, sweat and tears

To many in the United States, it seemed a foregone conclusion that Churchill would win the British general election. The Leader of the Opposition, Clement Attlee, was virtually unknown to most Americans.

23 May 1945, Cy Hungerford, *Pittsburgh Post-Gazette* (Philadelphia, US)

The hat trick

In order to make his new caretaker government as widely representative as possible, Churchill gave posts to National Liberal MPs such as Leslie Hore-Belisha, Ernest Brown and Sir John Simon, who are seen here hitching a lift. On 26 May, Churchill gave his first campaign speech in his Epping constituency. He asked that the caretaker government be returned to power as 'we shall take very good care of everything that affects the welfare of Britain and all classes of Britain'.

24 May 1945, Victor Weisz (Vicky), *News Chronicle*

The Conservative press conveyed the belief that Labour did not have 'anyone of their number who could rival Churchill in prestige or popular appeal'. They considered Attlee to be 'scarcely an imposing or inspiring figure' and compared his appeal to that of Bevin and Herbert Morrison, the Deputy Leader of the Labour Party. The *Daily Sketch* noted how 'polite and mildly enthusiastic was [the applause] accorded the conventional address of Attlee' compared to the applause given to the stirring conference speeches of Bevin and Morrison.

25 May 1945, Cyril Price (Kim), *Daily Sketch*

Fraternisation before the fight?

Churchill invited Attlee to accompany him to any Big Three conference held during the election campaign. This showed a dramatic demonstration of British unity on foreign policy, and a desire to have all opinions inform the post-war order. Attlee would, in fact, attend the Potsdam conference, the last meeting of the Big Three, held in July 1945.

29 May 1945, George Middleton, *Birmingham Gazette*

No change

Churchill made a costly political mistake in his broadcast of 4 June. Hearing of the intimidations, executions and political crackdowns that were now happening in Soviet-controlled Poland and Romania, Churchill was concerned about the spread of socialism. In his broadcast, Churchill claimed a Labour government would have to 'fall back on some form of Gestapo . . . and this would nip opinion in the bud; it would stop criticism as it reared its head, and it would gather all the power to the supreme party.' He also warned that socialism 'was inseparably interwoven with totalitarianism' and threatened freedom 'in all its forms'. Attlee sarcastically thanked him for showing voters the difference between Churchill the war leader and the party leader.

7 June 1945, George Butterworth, *Daily Dispatch*

'Mind that mine!'

The San Francisco conference (officially the United Nations Conference on International Organisation) brought together representatives from fifty nations to discuss and sign the United Nations Charter. It was proposed that the five permanent members of the Security Council (Britain, the US, the Soviet Union, China and France) would have veto power, but several countries wanted to reduce the power of the veto in case one of the permanent members threatened another nation. The 'Big Five' got their way. According to the *People*, the agreement to retain the veto 'is by far the best and most important news of the past week . . . "Man o' the People" is no tipster, but as an ordinary student of international "form" he believes that these developments show a marked improvement in the running of World Affairs.'

10 June 1945, George Frederick Shilling, *People*

All those in favour please signify in the usual manner

Churchill's popularity remained enormous, confirmed by the huge crowds that cheered him at every point on his election tour around the country. Even though opinion polls showed a significant swing towards Labour, it was widely anticipated by the media that the Conservatives would be returned to power. The *Manchester Guardian* went as far as to say that 'the chances of Labour sweeping the country and obtaining a clear majority ... are pretty remote'. Churchill, however, was less convinced. In his broadcast on 30 June, he reminded the electorate that voting for Labour or the Liberal Party would mean 'at the same time voting for my dismissal from power'.

1 July 1945, J. C. Walker, *Western Mail*

Three faces east

It was announced that both Churchill and Attlee would meet Stalin and Truman at the Potsdam conference in Berlin, starting on 17 July. During the conference, the Soviets reaffirmed their promise to declare war on Japan (although this didn't officially happen until 8 August). In addition, Britain, the US and China (represented by Chiang Kai-shek) issued the Potsdam Declaration, which gave an ultimatum to Japan to surrender or 'meet prompt and utter destruction' – although there was no mention of what this would entail. Japan did not respond.

2 July 1945, Tom Little, *New York Times* (US)

It's in your hands

The Conservatives still considered Churchill's popularity their trump card and, in the days before the election, billboards around the country carried huge photographs of the Prime Minister with the caption, 'Help him finish the job. Vote National.' Conservative Party organisers even thought it necessary to exhort their supporters not to stay away from the polling booths through overconfidence.

2 July 1945, William Furnival, *Lancashire Daily Post*

Dangerous corner

Despite the criticism of his 'Gestapo' speech, Churchill continued to denigrate Labour as part of his election strategy. One of Churchill's concerns was the power of the Labour Party executive – or, as he called them, 'unrepresentative persons' who would 'give orders to the so-called Ministers of the Crown'. This concern was exacerbated by the Labour Party executive chairman, Harold Laski, who said that the party would not commit to any agreements made at Potsdam until they had been debated by the executive. Furthermore, Laski had previously said: 'If Labour did not obtain what I needed by general consent, we shall have to use violence, even if it means revolution.' Churchill then used his broadcast on 30 June to warn that the party executive would 'strike at the root of our parliamentary institutions'.

4 July 1945, Leslie Illingworth, *Daily Mail*

'Hard luck, boys, you can't kick off until I let you have it back on July 26.'

There was a sense of anti-climax following polling day on 5 July, as the country had to wait another three weeks for the results to be announced. The extra time was needed to allow for the collection and counting of the votes from servicemen and women still in Europe and the Far East.

8 July 1945, Stephen Roth, *Sunday Pictorial*

Rendezvous

While at Potsdam, Churchill made a tour of Berlin, visiting Hitler's bunker and the ruins of the Chancellery. Ronald McKie, reporting for the *Daily Telegraph* (Sydney), described the scene: 'Inside the Chancellery, Churchill climbed over heaps of rubble and rubbish, poked into rooms, wandered round the huge banquet hall, where two huge silver chandeliers had fallen to the floor. The smell of his cigar was strong and clean in the long ornate reception hall where Hitler once strode, and where field marshals once hailed.' A crowd had gathered outside the Chancellery, and all began to cheer as Churchill left. He later recalled: 'My hate had died with their surrender, and I was very much moved by their demonstrations, and also by their haggard looks and threadbare clothes.'

18 July 1945, Ian Gall, *Courier-Mail* (Brisbane, Australia)

Japanese second front

At Potsdam, the Big Three received what turned out to be false rumours that Japan was about to surrender. Truman made a note in his diary for 18 July, referring to a 'telegram from [Japanese] Emperor asking for peace'. This was an unofficial attempt by the Japanese foreign office to ask Stalin to negotiate a peace agreement that would allow Japan to retain its pre-war empire and imperial system. It seemed unlikely that any of the Allies would have been prepared to accept such terms, even if Japan had opened formal negotiations.

19 July 1945, John Santry, *Daily Telegraph* (Sydney, Australia)

Dropping the pilot

To Churchill's astonishment, Labour won a landslide victory, earning 393 parliamentary seats in one of the biggest electoral swings of the twentieth century. Attlee was able to form the Labour Party's first ever majority government. Labour's manifesto had emphasised social reform, including commitments to affordable housing, full employment and health care for all. The Conservative focus on lower taxation, defence spending and Churchill's leadership was not enough to persuade an electorate eager for change and renewal in a post-war world.

The title of this cartoon, 'Dropping the pilot', refers to Sir John Tenniel's famous cartoon of the same name. That cartoon, published in *Punch* in March 1890 following the resignation of Chancellor Otto von Bismarck, depicted the great statesman as a ship's captain forced to disembark his vessel by Kaiser Wilhelm II.

27 July 1945, Cy Hungerford, *Pittsburgh Post-Gazette* **(Philadelphia, US)**

On 27 July, Clement Attlee returned to the Potsdam conference as the British Prime Minister. Churchill, who had gone to the King to offer his resignation the day before, remained in London. When King George offered him the Order of the Garter, Churchill declined it, saying: 'How can I accept the Order of the Garter, when the people of England have just given me the Order of the Boot?' Nevertheless, when someone spoke of the ingratitude of the British people, Churchill replied: 'I wouldn't call it that. They have had a very hard time.'

28 July 1945, Jim Berryman, *Washington Star* (Washington DC, US)

Two Churchills

The British people rejected Churchill as a peacetime prime minister but lauded him as the man who had won the war. This cartoon fuses a popular view of Churchill, while at the same time making an acute historical judgement. It would be difficult to better this cartoon as a way of remembering the British electorate's gratitude to Churchill in the war years, and its distrust of the Conservative Party and its policies.

31 July 1945, David Low, *Evening Standard*

Complete absence of saving faces

Clement Attlee's return to the Potsdam conference bemused both Truman and Stalin, who had expected to be negotiating with a victorious Churchill. The conference continued, nonetheless. During the talks, Stalin was informed about the successful testing of the atomic bomb (Stalin already knew thanks to Soviet spies inside the Manhattan Project).

On 6 August, four days after the end of the conference, an atomic bomb was dropped on Hiroshima. On 9 August, a second bomb was dropped on Nagasaki. The effects were devastating, with up to 226,000 people dying, mostly civilians. On 15 August, Japan surrendered. The Second World War was over. But the peace-making, which Churchill so hoped to be a part of, was to be done by others.

21 August 1945, Hank Barrow, *Omaha World-Herald* **(Nebraska, US)**

234

Post-War

Churchill served as Leader of the Opposition from 1945 to 1951. Three themes would come to dominate his work and rhetoric over this period: the formation of a powerful United Nations, the fostering of a more united Europe, and an alliance between the US and Britain that would provide a bulwark against Soviet expansionism. Invited by President Truman to give a lecture at Westminster College in Fulton, Missouri, on 5 March, Churchill used his speech to warn: 'From Stettin in the Baltic to Trieste in the Adriatic, an iron curtain has descended across the Continent.' He claimed that this territory was subject to an 'increasing measure of control from Moscow'. This was 'certainly not the liberated Europe we fought to build up. Nor is it one which contains the essentials of permanent peace.'

7 March 1946, W. H. Woodburn (Hengest), *Manchester Evening News*

(left flag) 'Iron Curtain Over Europe!'
(right flag) 'Anglo-Saxons must rule the world!'

In reaction to Churchill's speech, Stalin gave an interview to *Pravda* in which he labelled Churchill a 'warmonger'. The speech was, according to Stalin, 'a dangerous act, calculated to sow the seeds of discord among the allied states . . . In essence Mr Churchill and his friends in England and the USA have presented the non-English-speaking nations with something like an ultimatum: recognise our dominance voluntarily and then all will be in order; in the contrary case, war is inevitable.' The battle lines of the Cold War were already being drawn.

12 March 1946, Herbert McClintock,
Tribune (Sydney, Australia)

Efimov drew this cartoon following Stalin's interview in which he had said that 'Mr Churchill and his friends bear a striking resemblance to Hitler and his friends', but Efimov felt conflicted in doing so. 'I was often impressed by Churchill,' the cartoonist later wrote, 'by his will, by his wonderful oratory talent, his jokes. I really liked him. And then it was announced that he was our enemy, and we had to draw cartoons about him . . . when I drew him looking in the mirror and seeing a reflection of Hitler, that was, for me, not convincing and not pleasant. I realised that Hitler was a real Fascist enemy, and that Churchill was a political giant.'

14 March 1946, Boris Efimov, *Izvestia* (Moscow, Soviet Union)

The Master-planner

'Here are the four main pillars of the World Temple of Peace.'
– Mr. Churchill

Churchill was one of the first leaders to call for a 'United States of Europe' to prevent the brutalities of the two world wars from reoccurring, and to advance a future of peace and prosperity. In a speech delivered at the Royal Albert Hall, London, on 14 May, Churchill said that, 'If the people of Europe resolve to come together and work together for mutual advantage, to exchange blessings instead of curses, they still have it in their power to sweep away the horrors and miseries which surround them, and to allow the streams of freedom, happiness and abundance to begin again their healing flow. This is the supreme opportunity, and if it be cast away, no one can predict that it will ever return or what the resulting catastrophe will be.'

17 May 1947, William Furnival, *Lancashire Daily Post*

Beautiful prospect, Clem!

Clement Attlee's Labour Government had transformed Britain since its election in 1945, with the establishment of the welfare state, the nationalisation of several industries, and the introduction of the National Heath Service. But continued rationing and the poor state of the economy drained away support from the Government, and Attlee was only returned at the 1950 General Election by a slender majority of five. With the likelihood of another election just around the corner, Winston Churchill believed just 'one more push' would return him to Downing Street.

27 February 1950, Will Mahony, *Daily Telegraph* (Sydney, Australia)

In 1953 Churchill became a knight when he accepted the Order of the Garter at the request of Queen Elizabeth II. That same year he also won the Nobel Prize in Literature 'for his mastery of historical and biographical description as well as for brilliant oratory in defending exalted human values'. More than 2,000 readers of the *Sunday Times* applied for reproductions of this cartoon. The newspaper also used it as a cover for the birthday card they sent to Churchill.

29 November 1953, Sidney Strube, *Sunday Times*

*Tory Conference, 1974. 'Why, I remember Tony as an up-and-coming
Deputy Prime Minister when I was a Young Conservative.'*

In 1951 Winston Churchill won his first general election. The Labour Party won the popular vote, but the Conservatives won 321 parliamentary seats to Labour's 295, and Churchill once again became Prime Minister at the age of seventy-six. Anthony Eden returned to office as Foreign Secretary and was also designated Deputy Prime Minister. But there was much scrutiny during Churchill's second premiership of when he would step aside to allow a successor to take the helm. Churchill's desire to hold on to the top job, even after his stroke in June 1953, caused his relationship with Eden to deteriorate.

8 November 1954, Michael Cummings, *Daily Express*

'One man in his time plays many parts.'

The caption for this cartoon is taken from Jaques' speech in Shakespeare's *As You Like It*, and provides an apt description of Churchill's varied and momentous career. From his early days as soldier and war correspondent, through to First Lord of the Admiralty, Chancellor, Prime Minister and war leader, he had worn many hats in his time. This cartoon was published on Churchill's eightieth birthday. He was, at the time, pushing for a four-power conference to be held with the new leaders of Soviet Union (following Stalin's death) in the hope it would bring an end to the Cold War. But it was not to be while he was in power. On 5 April 1955, Churchill resigned his post and Anthony Eden became Prime Minister. His fifty-four-year career in politics had come to an end. In a letter to Queen Elizabeth in the following days, Churchill wrote: 'I have done my best.'

30 November 1954, Victor Weisz (Vicky), *Daily Mirror*